SAVVY MAGNETISM

with

DARK PSYCHOLOGY & MANIPULATION

How to Recognize Manipulation, Protect Yourself against it,
and Ethically Use Persuasion to Influence People.

KAN WELLS

Index

Introduction

Have you ever found yourself nodding to whatever someone else is saying, and later, you realize you have been swayed against your better judgment? Do you remember when you agreed to every request from that particular person? After realizing that you were being manipulated, how did you feel? It could be a better experience. Right? You know, when you are in such a situation, your actions are literally influenced by that person. Your words cease being yours. You tend to feel confident and assured that you have control over everything you are doing; however, sadly, you do not. You are just like a puppet on strings.

In our daily lives, influence lurks around every corner, and trust me on this: It's tough to avoid it. Either you are the influencer, or someone is influencing you. If you've gone through such an experience, know you are not alone. I have been there many times, and I know many others who have been there, too.

Let me share one of my personal experiences with you. In college, I was an active student. I was smart, too. Because I was the class president, my English teacher assigned me to help a new student and show her around. She had just joined a month earlier. So, I spent a lot of time with her, showing her our latest class schedule and introducing her to all our professors and classmates. I also gave her my notes and handouts so she could catch up. If she ever had any questions, she would come to me. And that is how we became so close. At this point, I still thought she needed my help, so she always wanted to hang out with me. But it turns out that that wasn't the case; there was something else I hadn't noticed. Because of the time we spent together, she became too attached. She was so possessive of me. I'm sure many of you can relate to such experiences.

It reached a point where she would become jealous because I spoke or spent some time with my other classmates. Whenever that happened, she would find flaws in these students' characters. Whatever she discovered about them, she would try to convince me not to associate with them again because of this and that. It was becoming creepy, but still, I believed her.

I mentioned earlier that I was an active participant in class. Well, that didn't sit well with her. After some time, she told me to stop being too fast when answering questions in class. She claimed that she was never allowed to answer the questions because I raised my hand too quickly. And she also started claiming that I was stealing her answers. I listened to her. So, I decided that whenever our professor asked in class, I would wait for some time before raising my hand.

After some time, I started noticing that she was somehow controlling me. And I wouldn't say I liked it, so I attempted to put some distance between us, but she would come to me, sobbing, and ask me what she had done to deserve a cold shoulder. I tried to tell her that I had other friends and had to spend time with them. She told me that if we were real friends, I would have to spend all my time with her. I didn't buy this. Then, we had a long conversation about it. And you know what she came up with as a solution? I have a well-drawn schedule for when I should be with her and hang out with my other friends. And, of course, giving herself more time than the others. This seemed too strange, but I accepted it. I never wanted to hurt her.

Some of my classmates came to me and warned me about her. I never listened to them. It wasn't until, as time passed, my grades started dropping that I realized the nature of our possessive relationship and how much it had affected me. I also started losing friends. This made me feel lonely. This wasn't good at all. I became worried. Because of that, I started growing tired of her possessiveness. Then, I decided to talk to her about it. She furiously said, "I knew it; you're not my real friend." I assured her calmly that wasn't the case. She didn't listen to me, and we stopped communicating after that.

After feeling guilty for a few days, I thought, *Maybe I went too far*. I followed her again after apologizing to her. I even allowed her to copy my assignments, quizzes, and exams. In addition, I did some of her reports and analyses. How much I have done for her is beyond me. It was exhausting, and I couldn't believe I let it happen.

I'm glad my classmates let me see things clearly. I never talked to her again. But this left me with some serious questions: *How can I recognize and prevent such manipulation from happening to me again? How can I protect myself from brainwashing? I know that in life, it's great to be persuasive. But how can we ethically use persuasion?* Now that I have grown, thinking of that experience and several others I will share in the following chapters, I can answer these questions. My experiences and those of the people around me have shaped me into a better person, and these experiences were my primary motivation for researching and learning more about them. This is the reason I wrote this book. I want to inspire you with the hope that you, too, can learn and grow from your experiences.

If you think that these situations are extreme or exaggerated, guess what? Whether you have reached that point in life or not, it's inevitable to encounter such situations. These manipulative dynamics can occur daily, on a smaller or larger scale, with your family members, friends, work colleagues, and partners. Maybe you've felt the sting of betrayal as someone you trusted exploited your kindness for their gain. Or perhaps you've struggled to break free from manipulation, only to find yourself drawn back by guilt or obligation. Just like how I had my friend, I know many of you have such people in your lives. It's not easy to understand what they are doing to us. I jumped out of my friend's boat early. But what would have happened to me if I lived up to her influence? What would my life be like? All I know is that I wouldn't be happy. I know of a friend who married her abuser. Can you imagine what it would take for someone to marry their nightmare? We have such people at work. Do you know what it feels like to work for someone without compensation? They receive rewards for the work you have done. But why become a slave to someone else?

Fear not, for there is hope. With this book, you will arm yourself with the knowledge and strategies to recognize the signs of manipulation and protect yourself from falling victim to its insidious influence. You'll discover how to reclaim your autonomy and assert your boundaries confidently, freeing yourself from the chains of manipulation.

With this book, your decisions will become genuinely your own. You will no longer feel indebted to the influence of others. By the end of the final chapter, you can defend yourself against manipulation tactics. You will have all the freedom to live life on your own terms. You will be able to use persuasion in the best way possible—ethically. You will learn how to use influence to impact others positively. You will be a magnet because it will be easy to attract whoever you want into your life. Imagine building genuine relationships based on trust and mutual respect. With this skill, you are set to inspire and uplift those around you, making you a better version of yourself.

So, if you're tired of feeling like a pawn in someone else's game and long for the freedom to chart your life course, take the next step. Together, we'll learn how to detect the cues to manipulation, use persuasion ethically and to our advantage, and reclaim control over our destiny. Your journey to liberation starts now. Read now; your future self will thank you for it.

CHAPTER 1

Deciphering Deception

—

A Deep Dive Into Dark Psychology

Plato compared the intellect to a charioteer guiding the powerful horses of the passions (i.e., he gave it both the power of perception and the power of control).

– RAYMOND CATTELL

The Dark Psychology Triad

Before going into dark psychology, let's first understand what psychology means. Well, this is when you study how people behave and how they socially interact amongst themselves. It involves understanding both their mind and thoughts. Now, what is dark psychology? It's pretty simple. You just need to understand someone can use psychological principles and tactics to manipulate another person by influencing their action and perceptions. These people may use different maneuvers, motivations, manipulations, persuasion, and compulsion to achieve their goals.

Take, for example, someone trying to get you to do something you don't want to do by playing mind games or making you feel bad about yourself. That's precisely what dark psychology looks at. Someone can look for your weakness; they will capitalize on it in a way that will make you feel they are the only solution. Then, what will happen next? You will give them whatever they ask for.

It involves lying, cheating, and even hurting others to get what one wants. It is a very controversial field because it can be used for good and evil reasons. But there is no denying that this kind of psychology can be a powerful tool for those who know how to use it.

While it can be used for evil purposes, some use it for more positive reasons.

For example, therapists may use it to help patients overcome their fears and phobias. In other cases, police officers can use manipulative tricks to get confessions from criminals.

Is it true that dark psychology offers some benefits? Yes, only if you are not using it to hurt others. Firstly, it makes it easy for you to understand and be aware of human nature. This is because it often makes the reason behind the hidden or neglected darker aspects of human behavior clear and understood. This allows you to approach some social dynamics with more clarity and foresight. Secondly, with knowledge of dark psychology, it becomes harder for you to be deceived, manipulated, or coerced. You do not fall victim that easily. And this makes you safe from harm or exploitation. Thirdly, it increases your chances of getting into various fields that are reliant on manipulation, like law enforcement, security, or education. This is because these skills are really important when handling challenging situations effectively in such fields. In general, it can actually help understand why people do what they do.

For ages, those in power have used these tactics to control others, but nowadays, it's often linked with types of people who have these personalities: narcissism, Machiavellianism, or psychopathy. These three traits are what we call the dark psychology triads.

Narcissism

This simply is where someone feels they are so important over others and lacks empathy for others. Narcissism is characterized by the constant need to be admired and validated. Narcissists are selfish people. They believe they need special treatment and are entitled to everything they desire. With this feeling of self-importance, they may resort to mistreating others in order to get what they want. These people are so envious, arrogant, and resentful. This trait is mainly among public figures like politicians.

Politicians always want to attract attention everywhere they go. They love exaggerating their accomplishments, small or big they may be. And they tend to belittle their opponents. They may exploit others for personal gain, display a lack of remorse for their actions, and feel entitled to special treatment. Despite criticisms or failures, they remain steadfast in their belief in their own greatness, unable to acknowledge faults or accept responsibility for their mistakes. This narcissistic behavior can have several effects on their interactions and relationships, often leading to manipulation, conflict, and a lack of genuine connection with others.

An example of a narcissistic person is Adolf Hitler. As we all know, Hitler was the notorious leader of Nazi Germany. In many articles, historians have described him as charismatic. However, he was also a self-entitled, controlling, and manipulative power-drunk leader. He considered himself a particular person whose responsibility was to create the most powerful German empire. He lacked empathy for others. He was a dangerous, ruthless, murderous narcissist.

Machiavellianism

This is named after Niccolò Machiavelli's political treatise *The Prince*. It is characterized by cunning, manipulation, and focusing on self-interest above moral principles. He was an Italian politician. So, those high in Machiavellianism are often strategic and calculating in their interactions. These people always prioritize personal gain and power, even if it means ignoring or disregarding ethical norms or exploiting others. Such people are manipulative and deceptive in nature.

For example, a highly Machiavellian manager will always aim to climb the corporate ladder at any cost. They do not care about who gets hurt along the way. They may spread rumors and belittle their colleagues. They even take credit for other people's work just to advance their own careers. They can exploit relationships and situations for their own benefit.
Such people form alliances solely for strategic purposes. They use charm

and persuasion to manipulate others into supporting their agenda. In Machiavellianism, interpersonal relationships are the tools for achieving individual goals.

Psychopathy

A pervasive pattern of disrespect for and infringement on the rights of others is what defines this trait. Just like narcissists, individuals with psychopathy totally lack empathy and remorse. They often exhibit superficial charm and manipulative behavior. They also tend to be impulsive and aggressive. Such people are also deceitful and exploitative, and they don't, at any moment, feel guilty or empathetic for their victims.

An example of psychopathy is when a business leader willfully puts a dangerous product on the market to increase revenue, even when they are well aware of the negative consequences for customers. This executive may manipulate data, deceive the public, and ignore ethical concerns solely for personal gain. This person won't care about how others will be affected. Despite potential harm inflicted, the individual feels no remorse for their actions and may even view them as justified within the context of achieving their goals.

Harmful Effects of Dark Psychology

When dark psychology is taken to the extreme, it is seen in many ways adversely affecting us and the societies as a whole. It can affect victims either emotionally or physically.

- **Erosion of trust and relationships:** You see, dark psychology techniques like lying, gaslighting, and emotional manipulation can greatly affect the trust you may happen to have with other people. When you decide to use manipulative tactics on others, you are actually sowing seeds of doubt in their minds, and this will make them start questioning their own reality, feelings, and judgments, which will confuse them and make them feel insecure about themselves. What do you think happens next? Well, They will become emotionally distressed, and their anxiety will increase. In the end, depression will kick in, and this will diminish their self-esteem. This is what happens to those targeted by such tactics, degrading trust and damaging relationships, leaving lasting scars on both individuals and their stance in society.

- **Impairment of decision-making and rationality**: When exposed to dark psychology tactics such as propaganda, misinformation, and persuasion, it will be hard for you to make sound judgments and decisions. Usually, victims may find themselves moved by emotionally charged appeals, false promises, or fear tactics. This makes them act against their own best interests or values. When something like that happens, these victims will not be able to think critically and independently, paving the way for regrettable choices and feelings of guilt.

- **Increase in aggression and violence:** As I have mentioned above, if you are someone who engages in dark psychology, you tend to lack empathy, remorse, or even moral conscience. This makes you exploit others for personal gain without putting into consideration what the consequences of your actions would be. You do not care if someone is hurt or not. And this is all because of your sense of entitlement, superiority, or narcissism. Other people's rights and emotions are not your concern since you view other people as a mere means to an end. This kind of dehumanization can lead to antisocial behavior, criminal acts, or even extreme violence.

Recognize Toxic Manipulation

It may be a fact that it can really be hard to know that someone is manipulating you, but there are many red flags you can easily recognize. If you are aware of these signs, it may be hard for someone to actually continue manipulating you. You would realize and jump out of it before it gets serious. Some of these signs include the following:

In Toxic Relationships

There are many ways you can be manipulated in a relationship. The following are some key indicators to watch out for:

- **Controlling behavior:** This is where someone exerts excessive influence over you and dictates your actions, decisions, or even your thoughts. Imagine you're in a relationship where your partner constantly checks your phone without your permission, monitors who you talk to, and insists on knowing your every move. They might even dictate what clothes you wear or who you can hang out with. This excessive control can leave you feeling suffocated and stripped of your independence. For instance, if you want to go out with friends, they might guilt-trip you or become angry, making you feel guilty for wanting to spend time away from them.

- **Emotional abuse:** In this kind of manipulation, you can have a subtle yet profoundly damaging experience. Your partner may use actions or words that can systematically undermine your self-worth and make you lose confidence. They may criticize everything you do or even play mind games with you. They do this just to make you feel insecure and dependent on them. They may use statements like, "You're so useless, you can't do anything right" or, "Nobody else would put up with you like I do." This will make you feel helpless.

- **Gaslighting:** When you are in a relationship with a gaslighter, your perception of reality may change. You may start doubting your own sanity or memories. Gaslighters will always deny or downplay their harmful actions. They will then shift the blame onto you, and guess what? This will make you question your own thoughts and experiences. For example, when you get into an argument with your partner, and they make hurtful statements about you, after some time, when everything has cooled off, you confront them about what they said, and they will deny it. They may say, "I never said that; you must be imagining things" or, "You're overreacting as usual." This would make you question whether you heard them correctly or if you're overreacting.

In Workplace Dynamics

A workplace is one of the most common environments where manipulating is all around the corner. Anyone above your position can easily manipulate you. In such an environment, these are some of the signs you can use to tell someone is manipulating you:

- **Manipulation by superiors:** Sometimes, those in positions of authority might want to use manipulation to exert control or achieve their own goals at the expense of other members. For instance, they might say things like, "I thought I could rely on you to get this done," subtly implying that you're letting them down if you refuse. This manipulation tactic aims to exert control over you and exploit your willingness to please authority figures. In another scenario, your boss might manipulate you into working overtime by downplaying the impact on your personal life and emphasizing the importance of the task at hand. Even though you may not want to, you may feel forced to follow through out of fear of retaliation or a desire to keep good ties with your boss.

- **Toxic office politics:** In some workplaces, individuals engage in power struggles, backstabbing, or spreading rumors to gain an advantage. This involves deceit and manipulation. For example, a colleague might subtly manipulate you into excluding another team member during a team project by highlighting their perceived flaws or mistakes. They might appeal to your desire for recognition or advancement within the team, subtly leveraging your ambitions to serve their own interests. This manipulation tactic creates division and mistrust among coworkers, ultimately undermining teamwork and productivity.

- **Exploitation of employees:** This occurs when employers or higher positions take advantage of their employees for personal gain, often disregarding their welfare or rights. For instance, a startup might lure talented individuals with the promise of equity and future leadership roles, only to overwork them with unrealistic deadlines and minimal compensation. Employees are locked into a cycle of exploitation despite promises of future benefits, and many are afraid to speak up for fear of losing their job opportunities. In some cases, employers might manipulate employees by gaslighting them into believing their concerns are unfounded or exaggerated, dismissing legitimate grievances as signs of incompetence or disloyalty. This manipulation tactic erodes trust and loyalty within the organization, leading to high turnover rates and a toxic work culture characterized by resentment and disillusionment.

In Your Everyday Activities

In your day-to-day life, you may be manipulated by your friends, family members, or even strangers. These are some of the signs you can use:

- **Social settings:** Parties, gatherings, and social events can be breeding grounds for manipulation. Consider a scenario where you attend a party and strike up a conversation with someone who seems friendly and approachable. As the conversation progresses, they shower you with excessive compliments, subtly probing for personal information. Without realizing it, you may find yourself divulging details about your life that you wouldn't usually share. In this situation, the individual is using flattery as a manipulative tactic to extract personal information from you. Furthermore, they might strategically manipulate the social dynamics of the event to isolate you from your friends or acquaintances, thereby increasing their control over the interaction.

- **Online interactions:** The internet is a common ground for manipulation. It is where you can find both the good and the bad people. There are many ways you can encounter manipulative behavior on the internet, like during online forums and social media platforms or even through direct messages. You just have to be cautious with who you interact with. This could include someone pretending to be someone they're not to gain your trust or spreading false information to sway your opinion. Imagine you're participating in an online forum discussing a topic you're passionate about. Amidst the exchange of ideas, you encounter a user who seems exceptionally agreeable and strongly supportive of your viewpoints. Over time, you begin to trust this individual, unaware they're subtly steering the conversation to align with their agenda. Perhaps they start disseminating false information or exaggerating facts to sway your opinion. Alternatively, someone may create a fake profile in a social media context, assuming a persona designed to elicit trust and sympathy from unsuspecting users. They obtain your personal information by pretending to be your friend and using it to their advantage.

- **Professional networking:** Even in professional settings, for example, you collaborate on a project with a colleague who harbors competitive tendencies. Instead of fostering a spirit of teamwork, they resort to undermining your contributions and diminishing your achievements in front of superiors or other team members. By casting doubt on your capabilities, they seek to elevate themself and garner favor with those in positions of authority. Similarly, a superior might employ subtle threats or coercion tactics to pressure you into working overtime or taking on additional responsibilities beyond your capacity. These manipulative maneuvers create a toxic work environment where individuals feel compelled to comply with unreasonable demands out of fear or insecurity. Recognizing such behavior as manipulation is crucial in safeguarding your professional integrity and well-being.

Psychology Behind Manipulation

But what drives people to manipulate others negatively? On the surface, it's an obvious attempt to get what they want, but psychologically, we know behaviors are motivated by deeper factors. The overriding element in chronic psychological manipulation is always an issue of power and control.

Dysfunctional relationships are some of the most common causes of manipulation. In such dynamics, you might find yourself trapped in a web of manipulation without even realizing it. Imagine you are in a relationship, and your partner constantly undermines your self-esteem, subtly questioning your decisions and making you doubt your worth. They might trick or coerce you into compliance or use gaslighting techniques to make you question your own reality. In such a scenario, your partner is trying to exert control over you. This often leads to a toxic cycle of dependency and emotional turmoil.

Some of the manipulators are people who are struggling with personality disorders such as narcissistic personality disorder or borderline personality disorder. Such people may resort to manipulative tactics as a means of approaching their relationships and surroundings. Take, for example, someone with narcissistic tendencies who craves constant validation and admiration. This person will do whatever it takes to ensure that all around them cater to their needs and desires. It's just in their nature and character. They just want to maintain their inflated sense of self-importance. Also, if someone has borderline personality disorder, they will try to manipulate others as a way of managing their intense fear of abandonment. They may use tactics like emotional blackmail or erratic behavior to keep others close. To such people, manipulation is a coping mechanism that is rooted in their underlying psychological challenges.

How we treat our children affects them when they grow. People who have faced some serious abuse—whether emotional, physical, or sexual—in their childhoods are more likely to turn out to be great manipulators. The impact of a history of abuse on the psychology of manipulation cannot be overstated. They may develop coping mechanisms that involve manipulation as a means of self-preservation. Imagine you grew up in an environment where you were constantly belittled and controlled by a caregiver. To survive in such a hostile environment, you might have learned to manipulate situations and people to protect yourself from further harm. This learned behavior can persist into adulthood and manifest in relationships where manipulation is a default mode of interaction. Also, the trauma of past abuse can change one's view over boundaries and consent. This further complicates the dynamics of manipulation in interpersonal relationships.

Key Points

1. Understanding dark psychology

- Dark psychology involves the use of psychological principles to manipulate others for personal gain.

- Examples include mind games, emotional manipulation, and exploiting weaknesses to achieve goals.

2. The dark psychology triad

- Narcissism: Individuals feel entitled and lack empathy, often manipulating others for admiration and validation.

- Machiavellianism: Characterized by cunning and manipulation for personal gain, often disregarding ethical norms.

- Psychopathy: Individuals lack empathy and remorse, exhibiting manipulative and deceitful behavior.

3. Harmful effects of dark psychology

- Erosion of trust and relationships: Manipulative tactics like lying and gaslighting can lead to emotional distress and diminished self-esteem.

- Impairment of decision-making: Exposure to manipulation tactics can result in poor judgment and regrettable choices.

- Increase in aggression and violence: Manipulators may exploit others without regard for their well-being, leading to antisocial and harmful behaviors.

4. Recognizing toxic manipulation

- In toxic relationships: Watch out for controlling behavior, emotional abuse, and gaslighting.

- In workplace dynamics: Be wary of manipulation by superiors, toxic office politics, and exploitation of employees.

- In everyday activities: Stay alert for manipulation in social settings, online interactions, and professional networking.

5. Psychology behind manipulation

- Dysfunctional relationships: Manipulation can stem from a desire for control and relationship power imbalance.

- Personality disorders: Individuals with disorders like narcissism or borderline personality disorder may resort to manipulation as a coping mechanism.

- Childhood experiences: Past abuse and traumas lead to learned manipulative behaviors as a means of self-preservation, impacting future interpersonal relationships.

In the next chapter, we shall discuss different techniques and red flags of dark psychology.

CHAPTER 2

The Dark Arts

—

Unveiling Techniques and Red Flags of Dark Psychology

The people who would like to manipulate and use you won't tell you your blind spots. They may plan to continue using them to their advantage.

— ASSEGID HABTEWOLD

Dark Psychology Techniques

As you prioritize your mental health, the ability to spot red flags becomes a powerful tool. This skill equips you to engage in more productive and rewarding social interactions. It empowers you to approach relationships and life's challenges with confidence and clarity.

At this moment, with the brief introduction we have had in Chapter 1, we can all agree that we have faced some manipulation in one way or another in our daily lives, and we understand the consequences it has caused. Or at least we have seen a friend, a family member, or anyone else experience it. This manipulation could have been from someone we know, either a politician, our boss, or our partner. These people use many tactics, and identifying them early enough is in our best interest to save ourselves from future regrettable consequences. Some of these tactics include the following:

Gaslighting

In the previous chapter, we briefly talked about gaslighting, but only in relationships. We find gaslighters everywhere in our daily lives. When someone tries to use this tactic on you, they want to make you doubt your own reality or sanity. When you tell them about how you feel about something or your experience, they will deny and dismiss it. This person will make you feel like you are being irrational or overreacting.

My coworker at my first job seemed friendly at first, buying me lunch and helping with assignments. Over time, he started criticizing me, saying I was unreliable and forgetful. Initially, I brushed it off, but it made me doubt myself. I began relying on him for decisions, eventually losing my job because it seemed like I couldn't work independently. He manipulated me into questioning my abilities, which led to negative consequences. I eventually lost my job because, to my bosses, it looked like I was not doing anything on my own. And they were right. He tricked me into this, and I ended up doubting my potential from my unawareness of what was happening.

Now, that time has passed, and thanks to everything I have learned, I realize that he used many different ways to gaslight me, and they are as follows:

- **Countering:** He used to question my memory, making statements like, "Are you sure about that? Why are you so forgetful?" or "I can't believe you can forget everything in such a short time." This made me look incompetent.

- **Withholding:** In some cases, whenever I explained something to him, he would pretend as if he did not understand anything. This would make me feel like I was not making any sense. He would say, "Now, you're just confusing me," or, "I do not know what you are talking about." I doubted myself a lot because of this.

- **Trivializing:** He used to disregard how I felt about certain things. He used to say I am too sensitive or overreactive in response to some concerns that I believe actually deserved that reaction. He used to belittle me a lot, calling me childish many times.

- **Denial:** Whenever something happened at work because of him, he used to deny it and instead place all the blame on me. He used to do this by pretending to forget what happened, saying he did not do it.

- **Diverting:** Sometimes, he could change the focus of a discussion by questioning my credibility. For example, he used to say, "That is just nonsense you read on the internet. It is not real."

Such people exist, and they come in many different shapes, colors, genders, and ages.

Emotional Manipulation

According to Dr. Harold Hong, a psychiatrist from Raleigh, North Carolina, "Emotional manipulation is a form of psychological manipulation in which a person seeks to control another person's emotions." Trust me, it is as bad as it sounds.

Using this tactic, someone will target your vulnerabilities and emotions to achieve their own agenda. It exists on a spectrum and doesn't always have malicious intent. Abuse can be covert or overt. For example, I had a supervisor who used to give me positive feedback just to reinforce and encourage me positively. In this sense, she wanted to influence my emotions to promote positive behavior and become an even better person. In most cases, this type of example doesn't signify malicious intent. But there are times when some people use it with malicious intentions.

Emotional manipulators are good at reading social cues and using emotional triggers to maintain power and control in relationships. Their actions are often calculated and strategic, meant to control your emotions and exploit your vulnerabilities while maintaining their innocence or concern. Over time, as a victim, you may start losing your self-esteem and independence as you become increasingly dependent on the manipulator's validation or approval. People use different ways to reach your emotions, including the following:

- They will purposefully say things to make you feel guilty.
- Someone may bully, harass, or ridicule you to make you fear them. You see, if you fear someone, you are more likely to do what they ask of you.

- Some may gaslight you to make you doubt your own perceptions and experiences, convincing you that something is untrue while making you feel crazy or wrong.
- Some may purposefully embarrass you repeatedly to make you feel ashamed.
- There are some who resort to blackmailing.
- Some may play you off someone else to create conflict that benefits them.

It is important to recognize such people and avoid them if you can.

Love Bombing

You have been in love before. Think about it: How did you behave toward that person when you fell in love with them? How did you treat them? I guess you used to compliment them. You gave them gifts and attention. Right? In so doing, you were gaining their trust. *Love bombing* involves "intentionally using excessive affection and attention to gain control over a new partner and make them rely on you more." Some people with traits like narcissism or those who are abusive may use this tactic. It's also linked with cults. But remember, someone might act this way without meaning harm. If someone is love bombing you, they might:

- give you lots of extravagant gifts, especially early on
- shower you with excessive flattery.
- declare love for you very quickly and often, even on the first date.
- want constant contact, like bombarding you with texts and calls.
- push for commitment fast, like talking about marriage early on.
- act overly needy and upset if you don't respond immediately.
- disregard your boundaries when you try to set them.

Love bombers want to overwhelm you and make you feel like you've found a perfect match. They might try to isolate you from friends and family to keep you close. However, they may become more aggressive and harmful after the initial affectionate phase—called idealization. They might withdraw affection, criticize you, or try to control you. This shift is called devaluation. They might go back and forth between being overly affectionate and being hurtful, using affection to make up for the abuse and keep you in the relationship.

Isolation

This is very common in relationships and friendships. Do you remember the story about my college experience with my new friend? She was using this tactic. In that story, she wanted me to cut off the friends she found me with for her. This may sound insane, but actually, many people do this. The person will come into life, and they want to be the only one you can depend on. They do not want anyone else to be as close as they are to you. This person may try to harm or threaten. They may also spread lies about you or the other person you are friends with just to make you enemies. They will attempt their level best to split you up. This tactic is actually a dangerous one.

Behavioral Red Flags

Manipulative people usually have similar qualities. You can easily spot these red flags if you know them, and they include:

Overly-Charismatic Behavior

A manipulative person is a charming and captivating individual. This is someone who will effortlessly draw people into their own circle. They possess captivating personalities. They can quickly join or even start a conversation with anyone. They light up the room with just their presence, and some of them are good with words. What you should know is that their charm is not genuine. They use it as a tool to manipulate others to their advantage. They use it to gain trust and influence through deceit or lies. You should be careful with such people because behind those smiles and charms are hidden motives and bad intentions you do not wish to uncover.

Inconsistencies in Behavior

These people are very inconsistent in their behavior and actions. Based on the situation or audience, you will find one of these persons displaying completely different characters. This makes it difficult to know their true character. One moment, they may appear warm and empathetic, showering you with affection and attention. They could turn cold and distant the next moment, leaving you bewildered and questioning what went wrong. This kind of person is very unpredictable. With this inconsistency, they can easily have control over any narrative, and it would become hard to hold them accountable for their actions. If you see someone behaving differently in different situations or toward other people, try to avoid them.

Lack of Accountability

A manipulative person is someone who deflects blame and responsibility for their actions to another person. They will never take accountability for anything. They are really good at shifting focus away from themself or their actions onto some external factors or other people just to absolve themself of any guilt. This person will make excuses repeatedly to rationalize their behavior and how it affects others. They will resort to gaslighting or even deny their contribution to a particular issue to avoid being held accountable. They do this to avoid consequences for their actions. In such a sense, the manipulator remains untouchable, and it may be hard for them to face any criticism or reproach. So, if you happen to be the one they are deflecting the blame onto, you face the consequences alone.

Playing the Victim

Such people often want to play victim to garner others' sympathy, empathy, or leniency. They may tell stories of how they suffered or went through a hard time. These people will unapologetically paint themselves as the innocent party in a conflict or crisis, even though they contributed most in that situation. These are people who will always want to be seen as martyrs in any situation. They portray themselves as helpless and oppressed to gain validation from others. In this case, their mentality of being seen as victims is their shield. They use it to deflect any kind of criticism or accountability away from themselves while eliciting compassion and support from those around them. This is like the way a skilled actor performs a melodramatic monologue, tugging at heartstrings and playing around with emotions to serve their own agenda. However, beneath the guise of victimhood lies a calculated manipulation. You should be careful with such people.

Manipulative Communication Patterns

One key component in manipulation is the way you communicate. The statements you say and the gestures you make at the person you are trying to control contribute a lot to how they will respond. Will they be hooked or not? It's all about your communication style. As someone who has been analyzing manipulative behaviors for such a long time, I hence realized that all the people who control others have similar communication styles. The patterns in their communications are almost the same. When you are able to recognize these patterns, it will become hard for you to be a victim.

Verbal Aggression

When you are interacting with a controlling person, they will always use demeaning language with the intention of belittling and intimidating you. You will always be on the receiving end of hurtful statements like:

- "You're such a failure; nothing you do ever turns out right."
- "Why can't you ever get anything done correctly?"
- "You're so useless. I don't know why I even bother with you."
- "You're a complete disappointment. I can't rely on you for anything."

- "You're so stupid. Being associated with you is embarrassing."
- "You're a screw-up; I don't know how you manage to mess up everything."
- "You're a total disaster, always making mistakes and causing problems."
- "You're a waste of space. You can't even handle the simplest tasks."
- "You're incompetent; it's no wonder nobody respects you."
- "You're hopeless. I don't know why I bother trying to help you."
- "You're so incompetent."
- "You always mess things up."
- "What's wrong with you?"

When they use such statements at you, you will start feeling small, and you may end up losing your assertiveness. With time, you will lose your confidence and, eventually, your self-esteem. You will start feeling unworthy. These statements, prolonged over time, create a power dynamic where the aggressor seeks dominance through verbal dominance.

Gaslighting Phrases

We have been talking about gaslighting here and there, but what are the common statements gaslighters use? These include:

- "You're overreacting, as usual."
- "You're being paranoid; there's nothing to worry about."
- "You must have misunderstood what I meant."
- "That never happened; you must be confused."
- "You're making a big deal out of nothing."
- "Stop being so dramatic; it's not that serious."
- "You're just trying to cause problems; why can't you be more positive?"

As they use these statements at you, they are literally sowing seeds of self-doubt into you.

Manipulative Praise

While praise is meant to motivate and inspire you, this kind of praise doesn't only give you that. It serves ulterior motives, such as control. Take, for example, "You're such a generous person, always helping others without expecting anything in return. It's amazing how selfless you are." This statement may seem optimistic and motivating at first, but it will make you feel indebted when you keenly analyze it. Because of the emphasis and recognition of your generosity and selflessness, you will feel more obligated to give and help this person, even when you don't benefit at all. These manipulative praises are just backhanded compliments or insincere flattery. Such statements include:

- "You're such a talented artist, even if your work isn't quite as good as mine."
- "You're such a great cook, although this dish could use a little more flavor next time."
- "You're so organized, unlike some people I know who can't seem to keep anything in order."
- "You're such a good listener, even though sometimes you talk a bit too much about yourself."
- "You're such a hard worker, although you could be more efficient with your time."
- "You're so caring and compassionate, although you tend to be overly sensitive about little things."
- "You're such a good friend, although I wish you were more available when I needed you."

At first, these praises may seem harmless on the surface, but they can affect your self-worth. When they attach conditions or qualifiers to statements, they maintain their superiority, as they keep you seeking their approval.

Conditional Love

This is where you are accepted or validated after meeting certain conditions. Someone may tell you, "I'll only love you if you do what I say," "You're not worthy of my love unless you change," "I love you, but you need to prove yourself to me," or "I wish you'd lose weight. I liked you more when we met." In such situations, your worthiness of love or approval is tied to an external standard or fulfilling the needs of others.

I had a girlfriend who used to say, "I love you, but if you don't spend more time with me and prioritize our relationship over your friends, I don't think I can continue this." In such a scenario, she could only continue our relationship if I gave up other aspects of my life. This put me under pressure because I had to sacrifice my autonomy and independence in order to maintain the relationship, and it made me feel guilty and less deserving of love if I failed to comply.

Psychological Manipulation Tactics

In your day-to-day life, you usually face very many forms of manipulations. People tend to use different tactics to control you. These tactics include:

Triangulation

In triangulation, someone uses a friend, family member, or colleague to say negative things about you or compare you unfavorably with others behind your back. Triangulation creates conflict and confusion in relationships. It generally involves indirect communication. The main reason behind triangulation is dividing and conquering or putting people against each other. Most of the time, the people who use this tactic have one thing in common: insecurity. So, they are not afraid to manipulate others just to feel secure in a relationship.

Usually, two of the triangulated individuals have limited-to-no communication between them. For example, Sarah and Alex are in a committed relationship. However, Sarah's close friend, Emily, constantly criticizes Alex and compares him unfavorably to her own partner, Mark. Emily frequently shares stories about how supportive and attentive Mark is, trying to imply that Alex falls short in comparison.

Unbeknownst to Sarah, Emily's comments plant seeds of doubt and dissatisfaction in her mind about her relationship with Alex. Sarah begins to question whether Alex truly measures up to Emily's idealized image of a partner. She finds herself seeking validation from Emily or comparing Alex's behavior to Mark's, creating tension and insecurity in her relationship.

Meanwhile, Alex senses Sarah's growing distance and insecurity but is unsure of its cause. He feels frustrated and resentful toward Emily for undermining their relationship, yet he is hesitant to confront Sarah or Emily about his suspicions. In this relationship, Emily is the third party, and she has managed to create tension and conflict. This is what triangulation looks like.

Silent Treatment

Have you ever experienced the deafening silence that follows a disagreement or conflict with someone close to you? In silent treatment, someone will intentionally ignore you and refuse to say a word or engage with you. It is some form of emotional punishment because it makes you feel isolated, rejected, and powerless. When you are on the receiving end of silent treatment, you will become guilty and anxious, desperately seeking their attention.

The silent treatment may manifest differently depending on the circumstances and the individual employing it. Below are some consistent signs that you may be experiencing the silent treatment:

- They deliberately and conspicuously ignore you.
- They either pretend everything is fine or provoke an emotional response from you.
- They suddenly stop talking to you for a long time, spanning hours, days, or

even weeks.

- They leave without informing you of their whereabouts or the time when they are returning.
- They remain unresponsive when you attempt direct communication, whether in person or through electronic means.
- They talk to others, perhaps even in your presence, while refusing to acknowledge or speak with you.

Fearmongering

This is where someone uses fear, anxiety, or opinions to influence you to do what they want. Whether it's spreading rumors, exaggerating threats, or issuing ultimatums, fearmongers just want to manipulate your emotions and control your actions. Fearmongering can take many forms, from subtle coercion to blatant intimidation. Politicians often use this tactic to influence their viewers. I guess you have heard some politicians saying that something terrible will happen if you don't vote for this or that. And that if you vote for or against it, you can prevent it from happening. As a result, you will wind up voting in favor of what the politician is saying to avoid the stated consequences.

When I was young, my parents frequently warned me about the dangers of going out alone, and they used to tell me exaggerated stories of crimes in our neighborhood. This made me fear moving out by myself. Their constant reminders about the risks of going outside made me second-guess my own safety. This tactic shaped my behavior and decision-making.

Love Withdrawal

Imagine how it would feel when the affection and support you once had from someone just suddenly vanished. This will leave you in doubt. Someone can easily control you with this tactic. Whether it's through passive-aggressive behavior, emotional distance, or outright rejection, love withdrawers seek to manipulate your emotions and behavior by using your need for validation and connection.

In high school, I had a friend who would stop hanging out with me just because I refused to do what they asked. Eventually, I would do it. It was just about playing with my emotions.

Key Points

- Make sure you identify all the red flags that may be involved to improve your social interactions and relationships.

- Gaslighting involves making someone doubt their reality or sanity, often through denial, trivialization, or countering their experiences.

- Emotional manipulation uses vulnerabilities and emotions to control someone›s behavior.

- When you are using love bombing, you tend to show your partner too much affection and attention to make them trust you so you can control them.

- Isolation is another way of manipulation, and it involves cutting off a person from their support network to maintain control.

- Behavioral red flags of manipulators include fake charisma, inconsistency, lack of accountability, and playing the victim.

- Manipulative communication patterns include verbal aggression, gaslighting phrases, and conditional praise.

- Psychological manipulation tactics include triangulation, silent treatment, fearmongering, and love withdrawal.

In the next chapter, we shall discuss the different ways you can use to identify manipulative behavior.

CHAPTER 3

Spotting the Signs

—

A Guide to Identifying Manipulative Behavior

Playing with people's feelings through manipulation is a way of controlling their hearts.

— RON PRAT

When you manipulate someone, you are essentially playing with and taking control of their feelings. When you are in control, you can easily influence their actions and decisions to your advantage. In doing so, you are exploiting and playing with their vulnerabilities, ultimately gaining power over their hearts.

There are many types of manipulative tactics that you can use, such as emotional manipulation, gaslighting, isolation, love bombing, and triangulation. Each of these types has been extensively explained in the previous chapter. You can use anything that you think is appropriate and easy for you.

Common Patterns of Manipulation

From my analysis of the different tactics of manipulation, I have noticed that there are many repetitive things they all have in common. Based on these common patterns, trust me, you can have anyone acting in your favor. These include:

Manipulative Language

You need to know that, as humans, we use language to communicate, learn, share values, and influence other people. When you want to manipulate someone, you need to use the right words and actions to be successful. You may use statements like, "If you really cared, you would…" to guilt-trip someone into doing their bidding. This is a tactic I am good at, and it has worked for me many times. Whenever I wanted something from a friend, I would use statements like:

- "I really need your help right now. I'm in a really tough spot financially."
- "If I don't pay this bill by tomorrow, I might lose my apartment."
- "You're my closest friend. I thought I could count on you in times like this."
- "I promise I'll pay you back as soon as I can. You're saving me from a disaster."
- "I understand if you can't help me, but it would mean the world if you could."
- "I'm so grateful for your generosity. You're a true friend."

By using these statements, I am emphasizing my financial needs and painting a bleak picture of the potential consequences if they are refused. Then, they would give me the money out of sympathy or pity.

Another way you can manipulate someone is through selective framing. This way, you can present information in such a manner that the alternatives are limited. This is mainly in political speeches or advertising campaigns where they pick and use data specifically in support and favor of their viewpoint. Another example is when advertising a certain product, they will selectively only talk about the benefits while ignoring the drawbacks, like costs. They will share testimonials from only satisfied customers, glossing over any negative feedback from others. What are they doing? They are making you create a favorable impression while minimizing scrutiny of potential risks or shortcomings associated with the product. If you are hooked, you will not be able to think critically about your decision to purchase that product.

Playing the Victim

As a recap, from what we discussed in Chapter 2, most of the best manipulators are skilled at portraying themselves as victims in times of conflict or crises. They do this to gain sympathy or lenience from others, even though they are the cause of the situation.

I have a little brother who uses this trick of portraying himself as the victim. He is someone you will find saying that he's unfairly targeted and unappreciated despite his efforts. He always tries to deflect responsibility for any wrongdoing onto others, seeking sympathy and validation for his perceived mistreatment. He always says, "I can't believe you're always blaming me for everything! You never give me a chance. It's like you enjoy making me the bad guy all the time. I try my best to help out around here, but no matter what I do, it's never good enough for you. You're always favoring others. I'm just trying to do what's right, but you never appreciate me. I might as well not even bother." But this is someone who is only blamed for what he does, and he is the main cause of trouble. This trick has actually worked for him many times.

Withholding Information

This is where someone hides or refuses to share relevant information or facts to control a situation in their favor or assume power over others. This tactic is very common in personal relationships, professional settings, and even broader societal interactions. In a personal relationship, you can hold information to have an advantage over your partner or avoid being held responsible. At work, I had a colleague who would refuse to share key information just because they wanted to gain a competitive edge or undermine colleagues. Such information included project details, strategic plans, or performance feedback, all of which, in the end, affected team dynamics and overall success. It's not actually good to withhold information; it undermines trust, transparency, and integrity in relationships and society at large.

Though you can also use it to control a specific narrative in a good way, my little children always used to ask me where babies came from. Someone had told them that when older people go to hospitals, some of them never come back. They had also seen their mother go to the hospital and come back with a baby. So, whenever they asked where babies came from and why some older people never came back, I couldn't tell them. I could trick them or jokingly ask them to guess. After some time, they made their own logical narrative that older adults go to hospitals to turn into babies.

Punishment and Reward Cycle

This is a widespread tactic used to control behavior. This works in the sense that someone is punished for undesirable behavior and rewarded for compliance. This cycle is based on the concept of conditioning, in which people change their behavior as a result of learning to associate particular acts with either positive or negative outcomes.

In this cycle, punishments include criticism, withdrawal, or threats to influence the behavior of others. The rewards could be praise, affection, or material rewards. Rewards are given out when someone behaves in a desired or good way as a form of approval and appreciation. On the other hand, when they deviate from the desired behavior, you can punish them to regain control and compliance. I use this at home: My children are only allowed to have extra screen time if they finish their homework before dinner. In this case, extra screen time is the reward.

False Promises and Flattery

When you make false promises like rewards, opportunities, or favors, you are making commitments and assurances you are not willing to fulfill. These promises are empty and only serve in your favor by making the victim work in your favor, acting in your interests. This tactic is common in relationships, business dealings, or professional settings. For example, a salesperson might promise unrealistic product benefits to close a deal, knowing they cannot deliver on those promises.

In flattery, you tend to excessively praise or compliment someone to gain their favor, manipulate their opinions, or exploit their insecurities. You may shower them with compliments to lower their guard, increase their susceptibility to influence, or extract favors or resources. For instance, some coworkers throw insincere praises to manipulate others into accepting extra work or covering for them.

The Four Stages of Manipulation

Let's imagine for a moment that you want to manipulate someone purposely, and you don't know how. You should know that there are four stages you would have to go through. It's all about discovering the victim, manipulating them, exploiting them, and maintaining control over them. With each stage in exact order, this is the process that most expert manipulators go through, whether they are aware of it or not.

1. **Scouting out the victim:** Before you start exercising your manipulation tactics, you must identify and assess your potential victims. In this stage, you have to carefully observe and evaluate the people around you to get to know their vulnerabilities or weaknesses. You can do this by socially interacting with them, analyzing their relationships, and gathering information about their psychological or emotional state. As a manipulator, you will always look for specific traits or circumstances that make someone susceptible to manipulation, such as low self-esteem, a desire for approval, or a need for validation. You may also approach and talk to the people in their circle to deeply understand or gain access to the target. For example, you might observe your colleagues at work to identify who is most likely to comply with your requests or who is most susceptible to flattery or intimidation.

2. **Manipulating the victim:** Once you have identified your victim, you can now go on and use the different psychological, emotional, or social manipulation techniques we have discussed in the previous chapters to try to influence

or control them. Some of the tactics you can use include gaslighting and playing the victim to erode their confidence, manipulate their emotions, or distort their perception of reality. You may also try to persuade them into compliance.

3. **Exploiting the victim:** After manipulating your victim, it's now time to start exploiting them—extracting benefits or resources from them. This may be financial exploitation, emotional manipulation, or the fulfillment of your own desires at the expense of the victim. You can do this in many different ways, depending on your goals or the relationship you have with the victim. For example, you exploit your brother's generosity by constantly asking for money or favors without offering anything in return.

4. **Maintaining control over the victim:** Finally, the remaining part is ensuring you maintain control over your victim for a longer period of time. This could include perpetuating the cycle of manipulation, reinforcing dependency, or preventing the victim from seeking support or assistance. You can use rewards and punishments, play the victim, or even use false promises and flattery to keep your victims compliant and submissive. There are many ways you can do this. You use techniques with them from their external sources of support or validation, such as friends, family, or colleagues. By doing this, you are making them more dependent on you.

Identifying Subtle Signs of Manipulation

No one wants to be under someone else's control against their will. It's understandable. But how can you avoid or escape it? It's simple; you just have to be critical and conscious enough. There are many visible signs you can identify it by.

Trust Your Instincts

Let's imagine for a moment that you want to manipulate someone purposely, and you don't know how. You should know that there are four stages you would have to go through. It's all about discovering the victim, manipulating them, exploiting them, and maintaining control over them. With each stage in exact order, this is the process that most expert manipulators go through, whether they are aware of it or not.

Notice Inconsistencies

You should be looking out for inconsistencies in the actions and words of someone. These people are good at deceiving or misleading people by changing information or a story to suit their own agenda. When you pay attention to such discrepancies, you can easily tell that something is not aligning with their actions. It's like in those relationships in which your partner always promises to spend quality time with you, and, after some time, you realize they always cancel plans at the last minute or make excuses for being unavailable.

Evaluate Intentions

Always take into consideration the reason behind someone's behavior. Is that person genuinely concerned about how you feel, or do they have other intentions? You should assess a person's actions, whether they are in your best interest or theirs. There are always hidden agendas behind good deeds and behavior, and you need to uncover them. You may have a coworker who is always complimenting you and offering to help you. At first, it may seem like they are trying to be supportive, but as you analyze this action more, you may realize they are only doing what they are doing for their own political and professional benefits, and their praises are intended to manipulate you.

Assess Reciprocity

Let's assume you have a friend who always comes to you for emotional support and advice during hard times. But when the time comes, and you are the one in need of their support, they are either absent or dismissive of your concerns. Despite your efforts to make the relationship supportive, with time, you will start feeling like they are taking advantage of you or are ungrateful. You see, healthy relationships are supposed to be based on respect, trust, and reciprocity. When you notice that someone does not respect your boundaries or appreciate your efforts, you should be careful with them.

Seek Outside Perspective

Remember the girl who managed to manipulate me in high school?—Check the introduction. Do you remember who noticed it before I did? They were my classmates. The people around you see what you are not able to see. If you are unsure if someone is manipulating you, try to ask the people around you— the ones you trust. For instance, suppose you are in conflict with a colleague who you feel does not respect you or undermines your contributions. You are not sure if they are simply using dark psychology on you or if you are simply overreacting. Before coming to a conclusion you are unsure of, you can ask your trusted coworkers for their opinions. This would help you get clarity on what the situation is, and they may also give you some advice on how to approach it.

Vulnerability to Emotional Manipulation

Have you been under someone's control before? Which one of your individual traits did they capitalize on and exploit? You know everyone has their weaknesses; these are the reasons you become a victim. Remember that the major aim is to control their victim, so what great manipulators do is identify and then capitalize on their victim's vulnerabilities; hence, all their work will be about that specific object or subject. In most cases, they will use guilt-tripping, gaslighting, and fearmongering to win trust. You need to identify these vulnerabilities yourself and work on them.

First, someone with low self-esteem is easy to control. This is because they find it difficult to assert their boundaries or even advocate for their needs. Someone with low self-esteem will always seek approval from someone else. Based on this, it would be easy for them to be gaslighted or guilt-tripped.

Also, someone highly empathetic and compassionate is more likely to prioritize others' feelings and needs over their own. A manipulator would find it easy to play on people's emotions to gain sympathy.

In times of stress, vulnerability, or uncertainty, you are more susceptible to manipulation than ever. During these situations, you want to be comforted, supported or helped to solve all your problems. So, whoever comes in the image of a helper can easily get to your emotions.

If you are someone overly reliant on others for approval, validation, or self-worth, you are likely to be a victim. It is because you tend to prioritize maintaining your relationships at all costs, even if it involves abusive behavior or someone exerting their influence over you. It is your fear of rejection or abandonment that makes it easy for any tactic to work on you.

Children and adolescents are not assertive enough to resist these acts and intentions. They may be particularly vulnerable to manipulation by authority figures, peers, or romantic partners who exploit their naivety, trust, and desire for acceptance.

Key Points

- There are different types of manipulation, and they include emotional manipulation, gaslighting, isolation, love bombing, and triangulation.

- To know that someone is trying to manipulate you, there are common patterns you can identify, and they include manipulative language, playing the victim, withholding information, and the punishment and reward cycle.

- Manipulation happens in four stages: scouting out the victim, manipulating them, exploiting them, and maintaining control.

- Do you want to avoid being controlled? All you can do is trust your instincts, notice inconsistencies, evaluate intentions, assess reciprocity, and seek outside perspective.

- You become an easy target for manipulators if you have low self-esteem, high empathy, face challenging situations, or exhibit codependency traits. Moreover, children and adolescents are considered easy targets.

In the next chapter, we will discuss how you can shield yourself from manipulation.

Shielding Your Psych

—

Defense Mechanisms Against Manipulation

Manipulating people always involves utilizing a half-truth or a lie in order to achieve a certain goal.

— RALF JUHRE

Based on what we have discussed in the previous chapter, are there ways we can protect ourselves? If so, which ones are they?

Developing Mental Resilience Against Manipulation

One of the most important skills you must have is resilience. In life, you are faced with all kinds of challenges, and among them are misinformation, persuasion tactics, and manipulation techniques, from social media to advertising to even your personal relationships. Your mental strength is key and a much-needed aspect to effectively overcome or combat these challenges. You shouldn't allow any of the tactics used to work on you. You should never allow anyone to get into your mind and emotions unconsciously. How can you do this? You must understand your vulnerabilities, be self-aware, and strengthen your critical thinking skills.

- **Understanding your vulnerabilities:** In the previous chapter, we talked about the different vulnerabilities that can be exploited. One of the first steps to building stronger resilience is recognizing and understanding your weaknesses. If you identify them, you are likely to be more aware of when and how someone is trying to target you. You will then have to avoid that person, and in doing so, you protect yourself. If you know you have cognitive biases, like confirmation bias or the bandwagon effect, you will see when you are being influenced by biased information or social pressure.

- **Cultivating self-awareness:** Being cognizant of your feelings, ideas, and actions, as well as understanding how to take advantage of them, is necessary for this. When you are self-aware, you know who you are, what you are capable of doing, how you feel about certain things, what you want, and why you tend to do what you do. With this skill, you will know when someone is trying to gaslight you, and you will be able to escape. If you receive a persuasive message or advertisement, you will have a strong feeling about what it is. You will take a step back, critically analyze it objectively, and think through whether your response will be in your favor. When someone tries to pressure you into making a decision, trust me, you will know, and you will be able to resist.

- **Strengthening critical thinking skills:** Critical thinking is an essential skill. You are able to evaluate and question everything someone says or does before making a decision. When you are critical, you can analyze arguments, consider all the available evidence, and then look through and weigh the different views or perspectives to make a conclusion. In this case, it would be hard for someone to make you do what they want. For instance, if someone comes to you with a sales pitch, you will ask as many questions as possible, request evidence of what they are talking about, and then evaluate the validity of the claims they may have made. You can't simply accept information at face value but will instead engage in a process of inquiry and skepticism.

Setting Boundaries and Asserting Yourself

Another way you can protect yourself from manipulation is by being assertive and setting boundaries. When you have boundaries someone is not supposed to cross, you give others limited access to your life and emotions. It would be hard for someone to say or do certain things to you. And when you are assertive, this gives you more concealment from manipulators. This means you can easily say "no" if you are uninterested in something or they have tried to cross your boundaries. You give manipulators no space to reach your emotions or tap into your weaknesses. If you want to be able to assert your boundaries, here is how you can do it:

- **Defining personal boundaries:** Boundaries are certain rules and limits you set in your relationships with others, and they should take them into consideration. These can be emotional, mental, and social aspects of life meant to protect your independence, integrity, and peace of mind. To set your own boundaries, first, you have to be self-aware. You need to know and understand your values, needs, and limits and recognize where they end and others begin. This may involve examining past experiences, identifying patterns of behavior that have caused discomfort or conflict, and clarifying what is acceptable and unacceptable in your relationships.

- **Communicating boundaries effectively:** Once you have defined your boundaries, you now have to communicate them effectively to others. You have to be clear, honest, direct, and assertive in your communication to understand and respect your boundaries. When you are clear, you tend to avoid any instances of being misunderstood or misinterpreted. Being direct shows how vital the boundary is, leaving no room for ambiguity, and when you are assertive, you send a message that the boundary is nonnegotiable and everyone must respect it. You have to do this with no fear of being judged. When you express your needs, you should use "I" statements. For example, instead of saying, "You always interrupt me when I'm speaking," one could say, "I feel frustrated when I'm interrupted because I value being heard." Also, you need to set consequences if someone crosses the boundaries. You may choose to limit your interaction with them, recommunicate several times, and, if ultimately the situation does not progress or improve, simply end the relationship.

- **Seeking external perspectives:** Sometimes, it may help to discuss your decision with a trusted friend or family member to analyze it and know what they think about it. These people can give objective feedback, alternative viewpoints, and emotional support during the whole process. They can assist you in exploring different approaches or solutions as well as identifying any blind spots you might have missed. From their own analysis of the boundary you are trying to set, they can give their perspective on whether your boundaries are valid and reasonable. This may increase your confidence and conviction.

- **Practicing emotional detachment:** When asserting your boundaries, you have to keep calm and composed. You must have self-control and try to see with neutrality. This is what emotional detachment is all about. When you do that, you can respond thoughtfully and assertively to others rather than reacting impulsively or defensively. In such a situation, you are placing your own well-being as the first priority instead of being drawn into others' emotions or expectations. This allows you to maintain perspective and clarity, even in emotionally charged situations, which facilitates effective communication and boundary-setting.

- **Enforcing boundaries consistently:** Once you have communicated your boundaries, it's now time to uphold them, but you have to be consistent. Regardless of any circumstance or situation, you must stand firm. When you consistently enforce them, everyone else gets a clear message that you are not negotiating about what you decided and that they must respect it. This requires you to be assertive, and you must follow through on the consequences you set when necessary.

Recognizing Victim Mentality and Overcoming It

Are you someone who always feels like you have no control over any situation or that everyone is against you? Or do you ever feel like bad things keep happening in your life no matter what you do? Do you find yourself always blaming others for every bad situation in your life? If you are that person, just know you have a *victim mentality*. If you struggle with this, even if there is something you can do to avoid a bad situation, you may not take that opportunity, thinking that you will not be successful. If you're looking to protect yourself from manipulation, it's crucial to overcome this mentality. But how can you do that?

First, you have to recognize your tendency to blame external circumstances for anything that happens. This makes you look at yourself as a powerless individual. It makes you think you actually have very little control over your life or the outcomes of your endeavors. What you have to do about this is be self-aware. You have to examine your thoughts, beliefs, and behaviors and identify patterns of victimhood or scapegoating. In addition, you need to self-reflect on your past experiences, analyzing underlying emotions and any challenging automatic negative thoughts.

Then, you have to start taking responsibility for the choices you make. You need to understand that you have the power and capability to make your own decisions and shape your destiny. When you adopt this mindset, you will take the necessary steps to achieve your own goals. This will positively change your life. In this setting, when you assume responsibility, you have to accept consequences for your actions, whether positive or negative. This will help you learn from your mistakes. You should also view any challenges you face as opportunities for your personal growth instead of seeing them as problems or obstacles. This will help you face them head-on as well as avoid blaming others for their occurrence.

Lastly, you will have to allow yourself to shift to this empowered mindset. By doing this, you will reframe all your negative beliefs and adopt a more positive outlook on life. You will become a more resilient individual with the new-found belief that you can actually overcome every challenge in your life to achieve your goals. All you have to do is challenge your limiting beliefs, become more confident, and focus on solutions rather than spending much time on problems. Moreover, you have to surround yourself with supportive people, can influence you positively, and seek out opportunities for your personal growth and development.

Building Self-Confidence and Self-Esteem

One of the vulnerabilities that someone may exploit is a lack of self-confidence and self-esteem. You should never doubt your skills and abilities. Deep down, you must acknowledge the fact that you can be successful. Developing a positive self-image and resilience is key to feeling optimistic and strong. When you have these qualities, you can easily recognize and effectively resist manipulative tactics used against you. What can you do to build a more confident version of yourself? Well, you can do the following:

You have to first be more self-compassionate. You need to be kind to yourself. When you are going through a hard time or having self-doubt, you should treat yourself with understanding and acceptance. You have to acknowledge who you are—your flaws and imperfections—without judging or criticizing yourself. When you make a mistake, you shouldn't criticize yourself. Everyone makes mistakes; it's normal. You should know that you are capable of success.

Next, you should celebrate your achievements, however small they are. You must acknowledge all your accomplishments, and this will make you see your worth, know what you are capable of, and understand your potential. This will strengthen your positive self-image and belief in yourself. When you do this, you affirm your value and resilience. This makes it harder for others to undermine your self-esteem. In this context, you can treat yourself to a small reward, like doing your favorite activity or buying yourself something you love. As you do that, you can reflect on the effort you put in and the perseverance that led to this achievement. Just enjoy the pride that comes with success.

Lastly, challenge your negative self-talk. Negative self-talk is one thing that greatly kills your self-confidence and self-esteem. This is where you criticize yourself or have self-defeating beliefs about yourself, your abilities, and your worthiness. In this situation, what you have to do is replace all the negative thoughts with more realistic, positive, and empowering ones. When you have thoughts like, *I'm not good enough; I'll never succeed*, or, *I don't deserve happiness*, ask yourself what you are basing your negativity on. You can replace such thoughts with, *I am capable and resilient, I have overcome challenges in the past, and I can do it again*, or, *I deserve love, respect, and happiness just like anyone else*. When you do this for long enough, your mind reprograms itself, and you become more resilient and positive about yourself. At this point, it will be hard for anyone to undermine your self-worth.

Be Confident

One of the most powerful traits that can influence how you view everything around you is confidence. This is something that comes from within. It nurtures your actions, decisions, and how you interact with others. Confidence makes you believe in yourself. When you are confident, you acknowledge your strengths and worth and have faith in your abilities. With this firm belief in yourself, it's hard for someone to manipulate you. You may be wondering: How can I build my confidence? It's not that hard. You just have to follow the steps below:

- **Respect yourself and your opinions:** You need to understand that your thoughts and beliefs are valid. They are deserving of consideration. You should know that you have the right to express them. By doing so, you are claiming your place in the world for who you really are. When you respect yourself and your opinions, it will be hard for someone to undermine you. They know that you understand who you are and what your worth is. When you value your views and beliefs, you will be able to have more meaningful interactions with others, and you will be able to assert yourself in the best way possible positively. Never forget that self-respect is a foundation for personal growth and constructive relationships.

- **Speak up when something is not right or fair:** A confident individual is not afraid to speak for what is right. If you notice any kind of injustice, inequality, or unfairness, you can use your voice to advocate for change. Furthermore, you should know that assertiveness is a key component of confidence. As a confident individual, you have to stand up for yourself and voice your concerns in an assertive and respectful way. If something feels unjust or unfair to you, just speak your truth. Besides, you should trust your instincts. You need to be open with your thoughts and feelings. Sometimes, it's just you who is required for change to happen, but you may never know until you do it.

- **Don't be afraid to take risks:** It's time for you to start pushing yourself. It's always an excellent adventure to face new challenges. There are many opportunities out there that you can seize. All you have to do is be courageous and determined. When you actually go out there to try out new things, it shows that you genuinely trust your abilities and are ready to grow and learn. You need to embrace that growth mindset. You can develop this mindset through dedication and hard work. When you are trying out something new, you should set goals that stretch your capabilities and push you beyond your limits. Then, you can break them down into smaller steps that you are sure you can manage, and lastly, take action to start achieving them, each step at a time. Along the way, remember to celebrate the small wins.

- **Stand tall:** Your physical posture significantly influences your inner confidence. Standing tall allows you to project confidence and command respect from others. Proper posture involves aligning your spine, lifting your chest, and rolling your shoulders back. This not only impacts how others perceive you but also how you perceive yourself. A strong handshake, open and wide movements, and maintaining eye contact are all part of engaging with people. Avoid showing signs of insecurity by not crossing your arms or slouching. Confidence is a powerful tool, and presenting yourself with strong, positive body language can greatly enhance your self-assurance and influence.

- **Know your value:** Living a purposeful and focused life requires that you recognize your contributions, assets, and abilities. Being aware of your worth gives you a sense of purpose and confidence. Positive self-talk and affirmations, which reaffirm your conviction in your own abilities, are effective strategies to combat self-doubt. On the other hand, embrace a supportive network of people who inspire and motivate you. Look for possibilities that fit with your objectives, passions, and values. Knowing your value gives you the ability to live bravely and authentically because it attracts events that naturally recognize and appreciate you. Accepting your value gives you self-worth and helps you live a happy, meaningful life.

Key Points

- Becoming emotionally resilient only requires you to understand your weaknesses, recognize any manipulation attempts at you, evaluate information critically, and set boundaries assertively.

- As you are setting your boundaries, establish and communicate them clearly, seek support when needed, and enforce them consistently.

- In case you want to overcome victim mentality, take ownership of your choices, reframe negative beliefs, and focus on personal growth.

- Become self-confident by having self-compassion, celebrating successes, and replacing self-defeating beliefs with empowering thoughts.

- How do you know someone is confident? They trust their beliefs, advocate for fairness, embrace risks, project confidence, and recognize their value.

In the next chapter, we shall look at the origin of human emotions and how these emotions influence your behavior.

CHAPTER 5

Insights Into the Mind

—

Understanding the Roots of Human Emotion and Behavior

If you discovered something that made you tighten inside, you had better try to learn more about it.

– NICHOLAS SPARKS

The Psychology of Emotions

Building on our previous discussion about *defense mechanisms against manipulation*, it's essential to understand how emotions affect how we respond to various situations, evolving over time to enhance our survival and quality of life. These are what I refer to as adaptive responses. When you feel fear, for instance, your body becomes hyper-alert, preparing you to either flee from or confront potential danger. This swift reaction is a quintessential survival instinct.

On the other hand, when you are joyful, you just love to engage in activities. Joy motivates you to become more social. As a joyful person, you have a good feeling about everything and tend to repeat whatever behavior benefits you. For example, you can become joyful when you achieve a personal goal or spend time with your loved ones. As a result, you will strengthen and repeat whatever led you to such positive experiences.

Besides joy or happiness, other behaviors, such as sadness or anger, which may seem negative, are adaptive responses. You see, when you are sad, you are more likely to start reflecting on your experiences. You are trying to discover what led you to such a sad state. This shows others that you need support during difficult times. In addition, anger greatly motivates you to change, which helps you defend your boundaries or address any injustices.

You don't need to feel bad about such emotions; they reflect what you feel deep in your heart. They are genuine signals that your body and mind use to guide you on what to do next accordingly. Understanding these feelings helps you have the power and the skill to use them in your favor and in a positive way. Hence, we can safely say that your response is thoughtful. For example, you can use your anger to make positive changes in your life instead of turning to violence. If you find yourself in any kind of situation, you are able to manage it better.

Emotions are processed and generated in a small region of your brain called the amygdala. For instance, any potentially threatening situation you encounter activates your amygdala, which helps you analyze and respond to the danger in the shortest time possible. This is how emotions are generated—fast and sincere in how you feel at that moment. In such a situation, your body responds with an increased heart rate, sweating, and other physical changes that prepare you to either fight or flee. The same process happens when you encounter beautiful and nice situations: The feelings generated are happiness and joy.

Your personal achievements or situations do not just cause your emotions. The people around you, the cultural norms, and the social contexts all have a role to play in contributing to your constantly changing mood. Do you know that you can feel different levels of comfort, expressing joy or sadness, depending on the company you are in? That's a fact. You will become happier if you receive support from your friends and family. However, if you experience social rejection, you may become angry and sad. Knowing how your environment affects your emotions helps you know who or where you should be.

Emotional Intelligence

This is the way you recognize, understand, and manage your own emotions, as well as the emotions of others. If you have high emotional intelligence, you can recognize and resolve conflicts thoughtfully and in the best way possible, coming up with informed decisions. Being emotionally intelligent involves having emotional awareness, empathy, and self-regulation skills. When you develop your emotional intelligence, it becomes easier for you to communicate with ease and improve your interpersonal relationships. This enables you to achieve greater personal and professional success.

The Connection Between Behavior and Emotion

When emotions are created, they are definitely going to change the way you think and act. When you are happy, you are going to engage in activities that make you happier, such as spending time with friends or pursuing a hobby you love. But when you feel fear, you are more likely to become more cautious, avoiding or steering away from the threat. Feeling anger signals that something is wrong or unfair, and what will you do in that situation? You will try to correct what may have gone wrong or stand up for yourself. For instance, you are in a meeting with your boss, and they criticize your work. In that instant, you became angry or frustrated. This will prompt you to address the situation by either trying to clarify your position or asking for more guidance, making you more aware of your decision-making process.

You need to know that the degree to which emotional experiences impact behavior depends on their intensity and length. Strong, intense emotions often have a more immediate and pronounced effect on your actions. Do you know that a happy person is very generous and sociable? However, the level of their generosity depends on how happy they are. And if someone is extremely sad, they may isolate themself and become demotivated. Also, the level of withdrawal or isolation depends on the degree of their sadness.

So, what is the impact of the duration of your emotional experience? If you are someone who has been stressed for a very long time, you are more likely to become a generally irritable person or a poor decision-maker or even develop health issues. On the other hand, your prolonged happiness improves your way of life by promoting long-term positive behaviors such as regular exercise or maintaining healthy relationships. Imagine you are preparing for a presentation. If you are intensively anxious, you are more likely to over-prepare or even avoid the task altogether. Still, if you are moderately nervous, you will be motivated to practice and perform better.

Even though emotions are expressed through behavior, they can be controlled. You have that power. When you are angry, you may shout or use physical gestures in response, while sadness may make you cry or be more enthusiastic. Sometimes, you tend to regret some of these feelings. This is because they may negatively affect your relationship with the people around you. In life, if you want to be successful, you need to learn how to control your emotions. You can use various techniques, such as deep breathing, mindfulness, and cognitive reframing. Such techniques help you to reframe your emotions.

When you feel you are being followed, you may freeze or retreat, then your heart rate will increase, and you may start sweating all of a sudden out of fear. On the other hand, happiness will make you smile in a relaxed posture and with ease. This shows that different emotions are associated with distinct behavioral patterns, expressions, and bodily reactions. You need to be aware of such behavioral clues to be able to recognize and understand the emotions of others. If you see your friend isolating or withdrawing as well as avoiding eye contact, what does this mean? It shows that they are sad or anxious. As a result, you will try to give them support or a listening ear. When you can recognize these cues, you become more empathetic. This strengthens and improves your relationships with others because it makes them think you care and understand them.

When you can easily identify your own emotions and those of others, you become emotionally aware. This awareness can make you respond to different situations thoughtfully, and this improves your emotional awareness. Before acting in a certain way, you need first to assess how those actions may affect the people around you. This will help you act accordingly.

Categories of Emotional Intelligence

There are many categories of emotional intelligence, and these include:

- **Self-regulation:** This means you are able to manage and control your emotions, impulses, and behaviors in various situations. If you can keep your cool under pressure or in a stressful situation, you have strong self-regulation. With this trait, you can adapt to changing situations. Social regulation also requires you to be disciplined in pursuing your goals, even if you face any challenges or obstacles. Back in the day, when I was training for a marathon, I was representing my community. Toward the end of the training, I experienced a week of rainy weather. This disrupted my outdoor training. I would have given up if I had never had any discipline. However, I resorted to using a treadmill and doing indoor training to keep me active as I waited for the rain to stop. This resilience paid off.

- **Motivation:** Motivation is what pushes you to achieve your goals. You are set to pursue success regardless of any challenges you find along the way. Being motivated means you have to be enthusiastic, determined, and resilient. Imagine working on a project that requires you to be intensely focused and perform for long hours. Despite these challenges, you will stay committed to finishing it and producing high-quality work. As a motivated person, challenges have no power to steer you away from your goal.

- **Empathy:** This is where you put yourself in someone else's shoes. If you are able to understand and share the feelings of others, you are empathetic. Empathy requires you to be an active and attentive listener, and you should be able to show genuine concern for how others feel. When you attentively listen to what your friend is telling you and, instead of dismissing their emotions, you acknowledge their feelings on top of giving them a supportive presence, you are genuinely empathetic. This strengthens your relationships and makes others trust you more. Your empathy makes others feel valued and understood. When handling situations, you have to be sensitive and understanding.

- **Social skills:** When communicating, your social solid skills help you easily engage in conversations. You tend to make others feel comfortable around you so they feel valued and heard when talking to you. You can easily make friends. Social skills are required in verbal and nonverbal communication, conflict resolution, and networking. You can easily establish yourself in a new environment when you have great social skills and your absence is always felt. By attentively and actively listening to everyone, engaging in open dialogues, and finding common ground through compromise, you are able to solve conflicts diplomatically.

- **Self-awareness:** This is where you can recognize and understand your own emotions, strengths, weaknesses, and values. When you are self-aware, you can know how your thoughts and feelings affect how you behave and interact with other people. It's hard for someone to pressure you into doing something against your will because you know and stay true to your values. Self-awareness makes you think through and assess your decisions in life; as a result, you make genuine and authentic choices. This is the foundation of emotional intelligence.

The Benefits of Emotional Intelligence

Emotional intelligence can help improve your way of life in many ways. First, being emotionally intelligent helps you understand and relate to others better. You become an empathetic person. Imagine your friend is unhappy about what has been discussed in a meeting. As someone with high emotional intelligence, what would you do? It's simple. You would look at and analyze their nonverbal cues. Then, you approach them and ask them if they would love to talk about what the matter is. When you do this with sensitivity, you show them that you care, strengthening your relationship.

Emotional intelligence also helps you communicate effectively. Remember, you have to think about and assess the situation before you respond, right? As a result, you are going to make an appropriate decision, and you will have to communicate clearly and respectfully. You also become a good listener because you cannot respond to what you have not understood or heard. Moreover, emotional intelligence teaches you to be more compassionate.

When you are compassionate, you can recognize when your friend is in distress and then respond with kindness and support. If you have a colleague with a heavy workload, you are either going to help them with some work or say some encouraging words to them. That's what compassion is all about and what emotional intelligence makes you become.

When you think through and evaluate something before making a final decision, you're probably going to make a smart one. There are many things to consider in this setting before coming to a conclusion. For instance, when you are deciding whether to take the job or not, does it align with your values besides salary? Does it make you happy? Does it encroach on your personal time? In the end, you will come up with the best decision.

Finally, emotional intelligence makes you stronger. You become resilient. Is it a rejection you have received from a job you really wanted? As an emotionally intelligent person, you evaluate this experience and find out what you may have missed. Then, you will move on with more knowledge of what to expect and become more focused.

Based on the benefits mentioned above, do you want to improve your emotional intelligence? It is not as difficult as it may seem. You can follow these steps:

- **Pay attention to yourself:** First of all, you have to be self-aware. You have to know your own emotions and behavioral patterns. How? Each day, take some time to think about what you are feeling and why you are feeling that way. Let's say you wake up every morning with exhaustion. Try to think about what makes you feel like that. Is it that you don't get enough sleep, or you're stressed about the day ahead? It can be anything. Knowing your triggers and the different behavioral patterns allows you to control your emotions effectively and genuinely. At this stage, you start journaling, writing down all your emotions and their respective triggers.

- **Use positive language:** Next, you should work on your language; try being more positive in your communication. Avoid using negative language. Always reframe it in a positive way to boost your mood. For example, instead of saying, "I can't do this," try saying, "This is challenging, but I can handle it." This improves your emotional resilience. Endeavor to use encouraging and motivating statements when interacting with others. You should learn to compliment others for their good work or show gratitude when you receive support. This builds a supportive and motivating environment.

- **Keep going:** No matter what challenge or obstacle you meet along the way, you have to keep pushing. This is possible when you build a resilient mindset. You know, life isn't a straight path. Challenges are normal, but should you let them make you give up? No! Setbacks are part of your growth journey. As you work toward your goals, you are going to make some small achievements; celebrate them. This motivates you to work even harder. Thus, surround yourself with positive and supportive people. When you make mistakes, lean on them and keep moving forward. That is what success is all about.

- **Watch your stress level:** Having emotional intelligence means you have to be able to manage stress. When you are very stressed, you may end up with emotional outbursts. You should devise means of keeping your stress in check, such as regular exercise, mindfulness practices, taking a walk for a few minutes, or simply taking breaks throughout the day. Such activities can significantly reduce your stress levels. This will help you have a clearer and calmer mind when making decisions. With your stress levels, you are always thoughtful when responding to stressful situations, and you always have control over your emotions.

- **Show compassion:** Lastly, be compassionate. When associating with others, make sure you understand and share feelings. When your friend is going through a hard time, do not judge them; listen to them, acknowledge their feelings, and show that you care. You can use statements like, "I can see that this is really hard for you." When you are compassionate, your friends will feel supported, and you will have a more emotional experience.

Key Points

- Emotions are the way your brain responds to situations.

- Emotions influence the way you behave and make decisions.

- What influences emotions are the people, cultural norms, and social contexts. This affects how you express and respond to them.

- When you are good at managing your emotions, communication, empathy, self-regulation, motivation, and social skills, you are developing emotional intelligence and more likely to be successful.

In the next chapter, you will learn to recognize and resist manipulation and a victim mindset through awareness, critical thinking, resilience, boundary-setting, and mindfulness. You will be empowered to maintain clarity and autonomy against cultural pressures.

CHAPTER 6

Resisting the Tide

—

Strategies to Combat Brainwashing

Ability is what you're capable of doing. Motivation determines what you do. Attitude determines how well you do it.

– LOU HOLTZ

Brainwashing Techniques

Before exploring strategies to combat this facet of dark psychology, it's crucial to first familiarize yourself with some of the most commonly used techniques. By doing so, you'll be better prepared to identify and protect yourself against brainwashing. Brainwashing is when someone uses manipulative techniques to change your beliefs, behaviors, and attitudes against your will. The actions or techniques are repeated until you start believing what they want you to believe. Various techniques can be used, but it would be hard for someone to use them against you if you can identify them.

Assault on Identity

This technique targets who you are. It breaks down your self-image and self-worth and rebuilds them according to how your manipulator wants them to be. This technique constantly attacks your values, beliefs, and sense of self. You are always told that what you are is not real or that everything you ever knew was wrong. As time passes, this tends to erode your confidence in yourself and what you believe in. As a result, you will start believing what your manipulator wants you to believe, as this is what they believe is suitable for you. Finally, you will pick up the identity that is imposed by the manipulator. This is how cults work. For them to initiate you into their organizations, they may isolate you from all your social networks and then intensely criticize and ridicule all your past lives while painting their ideology as the right path to take. With time, you may feel disconnected from your past life and end up adopting their ways and ideologies.

Guilt

This is where someone convinces you that you are flawed or have committed unforgivable sins. They will make you feel regret and think negatively about yourself if you don't do what they tell you to do. This is possible because you may find yourself not wanting to disappoint some people in your life. This technique targets your conscience. You tend to feel responsible for any negative feelings or bad things that happen in your manipulator's life. I had a girlfriend who always pointed at me for any shortcomings in the relationship. Based on the few mistakes I made, I was blamed for every single issue that came up. This made me feel like I was the only reason our relationship didn't end up working.

Breaking Point

This is where you are pushed to the point where you feel you can't take it anymore. This technique involves sleep deprivation, constant criticism, and relentless pressure. This tactic aims to break down your resistance and resilience, making you mentally and emotionally exhausted. At this point, you are ready to comply with what your manipulator wants you to do just to find relief.

Leniency

After they have pushed you to your breaking point, whoever wants to control you will start showing you some leniency to create a sense of relief and gratitude. This can be through offering small kindnesses, privileges, or a temporary easing of pressure. The sudden change from the harsh conditions you were living through to the kindness you are being shown makes you appreciative of the manipulator's gestures. As a result, you will become compliant with their demands. For instance, after working for long hours without enough sleep and food, your employer may give you hours of comfort. You may talk to your loved ones, sleep, or have some freedom. This will make you feel indebted to that person, and you may become more willing to cooperate, so you keep getting these small treats.

Compulsion to Confess

With this technique, you are pressured to admit to or accept guilt for actions you may not have committed. You are constantly tormented with questions and accusations of things you never did. Just because you want the torture to end, you may confess, and when you do, the manipulators use that to strengthen their narrative against you. This will give them more control over you.

Strategies to Combat Brainwashing

Now, how can you combat brainwashing? Whether through media, political propaganda, or social pressure, it is important to equip yourself with tools to resist such manipulation. The following are some of the strategies you can use:

Question Everything

If you are told or read something, don't rush into believing it; first, question it. Not everything you are told or have read is true. Some of it is meant to brainwash you. That is why you have to be cautious. Has someone told you something? Before you respond, ask yourself: Are there any potential biases or conflicts of interest involved? What is their motivation? Imagine you come across a news article about a new medical treatment. What you have to do first is find out if the article is sponsored by a pharmaceutical company that might benefit from promoting this treatment. Also, ask whether the information is supported by evidence. Are there credible studies or data to back up the claims? Furthermore, in case someone comes to you saying a certain policy will yield huge economic benefits, look for economic analyses and consult with experts to find opinions that either support or challenge this claim. Doing this makes it hard for you to accept information at face value.

Seek Multiple Perspectives

On top of questioning, go out and look for different viewpoints on any issue. This will help you come up with a more balanced and informed decision. Are you trying to understand a controversial topic like climate change? Instead of just reading information that aligns with your beliefs, try those sources with opposing viewpoints. You can also ask different experts in the field and listen to their opinions. Besides, you can read different journals and consider economic analyses that discuss the potential impact of environmental policies. This will help you understand the issue better, and you will end up reshaping your opinions. Moreover, you tend to avoid the trap of echo chambers, where you only hear views that reinforce your own.

Analyze Logical Fallacies

Logical fallacies are "errors in reasoning that undermine the logic of an argument." These fallacies have the power to influence your thinking. Make sure you try your best to analyze them if you identify any. This protects you from the possibility of being lured into doing something you may have gone against. Note that different fallacies can be used, and they include:

- **Ad hominem:** In this case, someone attacks the person making the argument rather than the argument itself. They may say, "You shouldn't listen to his opinion on education reform because he's not a teacher," or "You can't trust this scientist because they are an environmental activist."

- **Straw man:** This is where someone tries to misrepresent your argument, making it weaker and very easy to attack. For instance, you may find someone striving for better healthcare funding, and the response is, "They just want to give out free stuff to everyone." Such a statement is a straw man fallacy.

- **Confirmation bias:** This involves searching for and interpreting information in a way that aligns with what you believe in. It is confirmation bias if you only read news that supports a certain policy you believe in.

Having the ability to identify and analyze such logical fallacies makes you more critical when approaching different arguments.

Evaluate Sources

There is a lot of information on the internet, but not all of it is accurate. The accuracy and reliability of the information strongly depend on its source. Peer-reviewed journals, established news organizations with rigorous editorial standards, and experts with recognized credentials in their fields are generally more trustworthy than anonymous websites or social media posts. When evaluating a source, check its track record, transparency about its editorial process, and whether it provides citations for its information. You can also cross-reference the information with other credible sources. If multiple trusted sources report the same information, it's more likely to be accurate. Doing this will help you avoid misinformation.

Fact-Check Information

As I said, false information is everywhere, and not everything you are told is a fact. You know misinformation can easily and rapidly spread. That is why you must be skeptical of any information you encounter. You have to check its accuracy. For instance, if you come across a sensational news story on Facebook or Twitter, you should cross-reference it with reputable news sources like the BBC, Reuters, or The New York Times. In addition, you can use multiple fact-checking tools, such as Snopes, FactCheck.org, and PolitiFact, to get evidence-based analysis. Imagine you read a post claiming that a certain vaccine causes severe side effects in 90% of recipients. Before accepting this claim, check reliable health sources like the CDC or the WHO and look up the claim on Snopes or FactCheck.org.

Lifelong Learning

It is difficult to brainwash or manipulate someone with much knowledge and sharp critical thinking skills. You can achieve these if you keep curious and continue educating yourself. You can take online courses, read authentic articles and reliable books on a variety of topics, attend lectures and seminars, or simply engage in thoughtful discussions with others. This deepens your understanding of different subjects. It would be easy to know someone is lying to you when they try to manipulate you in the field you are conversant with.

Trust Your Instincts

Sometimes, you may feel something is off about certain information. Well, it probably is. Often, your instincts can alert you to inconsistencies or potential deceptions that you might not immediately recognize. This shows that you have to pause and reflect before you respond. At this moment, you have to conduct some research, fact-check, seek out more perspectives, and evaluate the different sources. This will help you come up with a more informed decision and defend you against being misled. So, if something doesn't sit well with you, don't rush into responding. Take your time and research.

Promoting Critical Thinking and Autonomy in Decision-Making

To garner success in life, you have to be critical and exhibit autonomy when making decisions. There are many ways you can learn to be critical and autonomous. This improves your independence and effectiveness.

First, you have to build critical thinking capabilities to assess data and persuade. If you want to make sound judgments and conclusions, you need to analyze and evaluate the information extensively. To be able to do this, you need to question the data that are presented to you constantly. You need to find out what the source of the data is, how credible its validity is, and the logic behind the conclusions. After critically assessing the data, you can make well-reasoned arguments supported by credible evidence. With these arguments, you can easily persuade and influence the decisions and actions of others.

When you engage in intense conversation and diverse opinions, you tend to improve your critical thinking. You know that different people have different views. So, by engaging with other people, you are going to be exposed to different viewpoints and perspectives on a certain argument. This will make your understanding of a certain issue broader. If you are discussing an issue with friends, you should always encourage everyone to share their opinions, even if they differ from yours. When they all share, you may have a way of refining your own opinion.

Furthermore, you need to be media literate in today's digital era. You should assess all the information you find online. You need to find out if it is pushing any biases or propaganda. Thus, you must analyze the news sources critically. Find out how credible the publisher is, cross-reference information with multiple outlets, and be aware of the language used—whether it's emotionally charged or fact-based. When you do this thorough check, you may find traces of propaganda techniques, such as emotional appeals and repetition. This will help you avoid biased information.

Moreover, you should make well-informed decisions based on your objectives and values. Before making a decision, you ought to compile pertinent data, balance the pros and cons, and think about the decision's long-term effects. Begin by clearly defining your goals and values. For example, if you value sustainability and are deciding which car to buy, research options that align with this value, such as electric or hybrid vehicles. Look into each option's environmental impact, cost, and performance to make an informed choice. Additionally, seek out advice from experts and those with firsthand experience. If you're considering a career change, talk to professionals in the field to understand the industry's realities. Use their insights to evaluate how well the new career aligns with your goals and values.

Key Points

- Manipulators use techniques such as assault on identity, guilt, self-betrayal, breaking point, leniency, and compulsion to confess to brainwash you.

- If you want to avoid being a victim of brainwashing, question everything, seek multiple perspectives, analyze logical fallacies, evaluate sources, fact-check information, do lifelong learning, and trust your instincts.

- To foster success, develop critical thinking skills, engage in diverse conversations, educate yourself on media, and encourage questioning propaganda to improve independence and decision-making effectiveness.

The following chapter guides you through using dark psychological strategies for self-improvement, emphasizing the ethical issues, pros, and cons of techniques like behavior modification and cognitive reframing, and encourages developing empathy and self-awareness to use these tools responsibly while respecting moral limits.

Mastering Your Mind

—

The Power of Mind-Hacking Yourself

Everyone wants to live on top of the mountain, but all the happiness and growth occur while you're climbing it.

– ANDY ROONEY

Self-Awareness Through Observation

As already mentioned in the previous chapters, self-awareness is an essential life skill for personal and professional growth and development. There are many ways you can master being self-aware, among which is observation. When you observe yourself, you can discover the patterns in your behavior and what motivates you to do what you do. You can develop self-awareness through observation in many ways.

First, be mindful of your feelings, ideas, and actions. You have to be present in the moment as you consciously observe your inner and outer experiences and with no judgment. For instance, you are in a meeting, and then someone disrupts, dismissing your ideas. Before you even think of suppressing and justifying that feeling, try to ask yourself these questions: What exactly am I feeling right now? Is it irritation, embarrassment, or something else? When you acknowledge and clearly understand your emotions, you will be able to make thoughtful responses that may not make you regret them later.

Once you are mindful of your feelings, ideas, and actions, what you need to do is identify trends and stimuli that trigger these responses. This involves looking for recurring themes or situations that make you react in a certain way. Do you feel stressed when you are facing tight deadlines? Do certain people make you defensive when you disagree with them? Identifying and knowing these patterns makes you aware of what triggers a certain response from you. This helps you know what to base your decision on when setting clear boundaries.

And lastly, you have to look deeply and critically into the reasons why you behave or act the way you do. These actions usually come from your beliefs, values, and past experiences. If you find yourself hating social gatherings, you should ask yourself why. Is it because you value being alone, or is it the fear of judgment that is rooted in past negative experiences? When you find yourself in a certain situation, and you are feeling a certain way, you need to self-inquire and engage in introspection: What am I feeling right now? Why am I feeling this way? What past experiences might be influencing my current behavior? When you do this, you may find out that your procrastination, if that's your habit, is caused by your past experience of failure. You never know until you try to get answers. You may also ask for feedback from others about how they feel about your behavior. Genuine people will give you their perspectives as they tend to notice some patterns in your behavior that you may not be aware of.

Psychological Self-Analysis

When performing self-analysis, never forget to first self-reflect and engage in introspection. You must always set some time aside and contemplate your thoughts, feelings, and actions. One of the most effective ways of doing this is journaling. Each day that passes, you can write about all the experiences you had and your genuine reactions to each one of them. Then, you can use this information to reflect on what specifically triggered these reactions or responses. You can actually get a lot of insights from this written information. This will help you find the patterns in your behavior after some time. Moreover, another method you can use is meditation.

An important part of psychological self-analysis is examining your prejudices and ingrained assumptions. There are various beliefs that you unintentionally adopt from your family, culture, or society. It's normal because everyone has these beliefs or values. But no one knows what exactly these beliefs are. To reveal them, start by questioning your automatic responses to certain people or situations. In case you find yourself feeling uneasy and uncomfortable around people from a particular background, ask yourself why. Is this based on personal experience or influenced by stereotypes you have been exposed to? Also, you can engage with these people; trust me, you will get different opinions on a lot of things you know. As a result, you will understand how different you are from them.

In addition, you should identify areas where you need to improve in your personal life. Remember, you have to get feedback from people around you. Then, you have to reflect on this feedback as well as your own observations. You may also use a journal to write down your ideas: the solutions you have come up with, the time duration for certain goals, the boundaries you want to set, and much more. This will help you in your journey of self-improvement.

Cognitive Behavioral Strategies

Cognitive behavior refers to "various mental and emotional health issues, including anxiety and depression." These behaviors have a negative effect on your life. They are obstacles in your journey to personal growth. When you are depressed, you can't do anything constructive. If you want to change your life for the better and you want to overcome these cognitive behaviors, you can follow these strategies.

First of all, you should overcome the cognitive biases that you may be having. These are the root causes of anxiety and depression. If you want to get rid of them, you need first to be aware of them. If you constantly engage in catastrophizing, always expecting the worst out of something, you are crowding your mind with negativity. In such a situation, you may find yourself thinking, *I'll definitely fail this exam and ruin my future*. This statement is a cognitive bias. So, to avoid this, you need to self-reflect. You need to assess the negative statements you make with questions like, *Is this thought based on facts?* or, *What evidence do I have that this will happen?* You need to assess all this negativity to overcome all the cognitive distortions like all-or-nothing thinking, overgeneralization, and emotional reasoning. You can start to question and correct these patterns. If you recognize them, you can reframe your thinking in a more balanced and realistic way.

After identifying all the negative ideas and thoughts, you can restructure them positively. You can replace these negative thoughts with constructive ones. Let's say you believe *I'm not good enough to get promoted*. This will make you less confident and eventually affect your performance. To restructure it, you have to first acknowledge it as harmful. Next, challenge it by evaluating the evidence. Ask yourself, *What evidence do I have that I'm not good enough?* And, *What accomplishments prove my capability?* This critical evaluation often reveals that the belief is unfounded or exaggerated. Then, replace the harmful thought with a more positive and realistic one. You might say, "I have received positive feedback from my supervisor and have successfully completed several key projects. I am capable and worthy of a promotion." By consistently practicing this technique, you can alter deeply ingrained, harmful ideas, leading to improved self-esteem.

Lastly, put cognitive-behavioral methods to use in changing behavior. Focus on changing both thought patterns and behaviors to improve your emotional health. One of the most effective methods you can use is behavioral activation. You only engage in activities that are in line with your values and interests to overcome negative emotions. Assuming you struggle with depression and find it hard to get out of bed, how can you use behavioral activation in such a situation? You must first identify the activities you love, even if they seem challenging at times, such as painting. You will then decide to break it into small and manageable goals, like painting for just 10 minutes a day. When you break it down, it becomes more approachable.

Besides behavioral activation, you can use exposure therapy to help you with anxiety-related behaviors. Let's say you are afraid of public speaking. To overcome this, you must gradually start exposing yourself to speaking situations. You can begin by speaking in front of a mirror, then to a small group of friends, and eventually work your way up to larger audiences. This gradual process systematically makes public speaking less intimidating.

Techniques for Self-Reflection and Self-Improvement

As a recap, self-reflection helps you better understand yourself, leading to self-improvement. How do you self-reflect effectively? There are many ways you can do this:

Journaling

Journaling offers you private space and time to reflect on your thoughts, emotions, and experiences. You can do this every single day, some days, or weekly. You have to set a specific period for when you will be writing. It could be in the morning to set what you expect to achieve during the day or at night to reflect on your experiences throughout the day.

One of the most popular ways of journaling is *gratitude journaling*. In this technique, you write down three things you are grateful for. They could be, "I'm grateful for the supportive conversation I had with my friend today," "I'm grateful for the delicious coffee I enjoyed this morning," and, "I'm grateful for the beautiful weather during my walk." When you do this consistently for a long time, you will start viewing yourself in a positive light.

Another technique is *stream-of-consciousness journaling*. In your journal, you write whatever comes to mind without filtering. This will help you become aware of your inner thoughts and feelings that you didn't know about. You can write statements like, "Today, I felt overwhelmed at work." From there, write whatever you think of; let your thoughts flow naturally. You will find yourself writing about specific tasks that stress you out or worrying about future projects.

Lastly, there is *prompt journaling*. In your journal, you have specific questions or prompts you have to answer or respond to. When you answer these prompts, you may be able to understand yourself better.

Feedback-Seeking and Processing

You need to know what people think about your actions, behavior, or opinions. So, you need to ask the people you trust about your views or anything you are doing or intend to do. You need to ask them to be honest. When you get this feedback, you have to process it constructively. Think about it critically. Do not interrupt or defend yourself when they are talking to you if they are criticizing you or have a different perspective from yours. Reflect on this feedback. If what they have told you is actionable, go ahead and make plans to address it.

Goal-Setting and Progress-Tracking

Then, you need to set goals, which you have to follow up on. You should set these goals using SMART criteria—specific, measurable, achievable, relevant, and time-bound. Instead of setting a general goal like, "I want to get fit," you could put it in a SMART way like, "I will run three times a week for 30 minutes each session for the next two months."

When you have set your goals and put them into action, you need to track their progress regularly. You can use a digital app, a planner, or a simple checklist to monitor your progress. This helps you stay motivated. If you realize reaching your running goals is hard, you may consider reevaluating your schedule and plan. Celebrate every milestone or achievement you reach, no matter how small. If you've managed to stick to your running schedule for a month, reward yourself with something enjoyable, like a new book or a relaxing day off.

Self-Coaching Techniques

This involves guiding yourself through challenges and personal development. You can use structured networks when doing this. I always use the *GROW model*—a technique I have used for many years that has turned out to be effective. It stands for Goal, Reality, Options, and Will.

1. **Goal:** Define what you want to achieve. For example, "I want to improve my public speaking skills."
2. **Reality:** Assess your current situation. Ask yourself, "What is my current level of skill? What feedback have I received?"
3. **Options:** Explore different strategies to reach your goal. Consider options like joining a public speaking club, practicing in front of friends, or taking an online course.
4. **Will:** Commit to a plan of action. Decide on the steps you will take and set a timeline. For instance, "I will join a public speaking club this month and practice weekly."

Another effective technique I use is positive self-talk. In this technique, you have to replace all the negative thoughts you may be having with positive ones. If you catch yourself thinking, *I'll never be good at this*, reframe it to, *I am capable, and I can improve with practice.*

Using Mindfulness to Counter Manipulative Influences

When you use mindfulness to counteract manipulative influences, it becomes easier.

Practicing Present-Moment Awareness

This is where you pay full attention to the situation you are in at the moment. This is the foundation of mindfulness. Practicing present-moment awareness makes you more aware of the people and everything going on around you. For instance, you are in a meeting, and someone tries to push you to agree to a proposal you are uncomfortable with. What you have to do is first be sure if they are being manipulative. How? There are some signs to recognize it, such as their tone of voice and body language. Afterward, instead of reacting impulsively, you can respond calmly and assertively or request more time to consider the proposal.

Detaching From Identification With Thoughts and Emotions

To be mindful, you must watch your thoughts and feelings without being connected to them. When you detach yourself, you can see situations more objectively. This makes it hard for someone to manipulate you. When someone criticizes you harshly, just trying to provoke you, you don't need to defend yourself or feel hurt. What you can do is keenly observe the criticism and your emotional response to it without identifying with these feelings. This makes you respond thoughtfully rather than reactively. Note that you have to maintain composure and potentially diffuse the manipulative intent. Furthermore, you have to handle these thoughts and emotions as if you were an impartial witness. Never let yourself get caught up in these emotions. When you do this, you can make more rational and less emotionally driven decisions.

Cultivating Inner Calm and Equanimity

You have to maintain your inner calm and equanimity to have a balanced and composed state of mind, even in stressful situations. When you are not calm, it becomes easier for manipulators to unsettle you and gain control. For example, you are in negotiation, and the other person tries to pressure you into a quick decision. If you are calm, you remain centered and think clearly. This helps you make decisions that are in your best interest rather than those that serve the manipulator's agenda. You can gain this calmness through regular meditation practice, deep breathing exercises, or yoga.

Key Points

- Be self-aware through observation, being mindful of your feelings. Identify behavioral trends and understand the underlying reasons behind your actions.

- To effectively psychologically self-analyze, you are required to reflect introspectively, investigate biases, and determine areas for personal improvement.

- Overcoming cognitive biases, practicing cognitive restructuring, and using cognitive-behavioral methods to change behavior are some of the cognitive behavioral strategies you can use in life.

- Develop emotional intelligence by improving emotional awareness, recognizing feelings' impact on decisions, and cultivating empathy.

- Engage in journaling, seek constructive feedback, set and track goals, and use self-coaching techniques for self-improvement to overcome manipulative influences.

In the next chapter, we'll discuss how you can interpret human behavior to predict actions by analyzing speech patterns, body language, and environmental clues, enhancing your interpersonal skills, and strategic planning through case studies and hands-on activities.

CHAPTER 8

Mastering the Art of Body

—

Language Analysis

It is not primarily our physical selves that limit us but rather our mindset about our physical limits.

– ELLEN J. LANGER

The Power of Nonverbal Communication

We usually use nonverbal communication every day without even realizing it. This is where we use facial expressions, body language, eye contact, gestures, and even the physical distance between us and others. In many ways, we communicate like this. If you are in a position to understand and master these nonverbal cues, it will be easy for you to connect with other people. You can easily convey your intentions and build stronger relationships because it shows how invested you are in understanding others.

- **Universal expressions:** These are facial expressions that can be recognized and understood across different cultures. These expressions usually convey specific emotions, such as happiness, sadness, anger, fear, surprise, and disgust. When you smile, it shows that you are a friendly and approachable person. However, it can be read as displeasure or concern when you frown at someone. All people from different parts of the world can recognize the same emotion you are trying to convey. It is important to read such emotions because it helps you respond appropriately to those around you. For instance, when you realize that someone's face lights up whenever you approach them, trust me, you will always feel encouraged to visit them. On the other hand, when you recognize signs of discomfort, you may either try to adjust your behavior toward this person or you may not want to visit them again.

- **Body posture and dominance:** Your body posture says much about your confidence, status, and intentions. Imagine two people approach you: one is standing tall with their shoulders pushed back and their chest out wide, while the other has a slouched posture. Who, of the two, do you think is confident and authoritative? It is obviously the first person. This is because their posture projects what they are or what they want you to think of them. The posture of the second person makes them appear small and submissive. So, you need to adopt the dominant posture if you want people to respect you and follow your lead. When you notice your friend suddenly adopting a certain posture, you can tell if they are feeling sad and depressed or happy and confident. If you see your friend suddenly slouching, you can know there is something wrong that is making them feel small.

- **Mirroring and rapport:** When you mimic the body language and gestures of another person, you create a bond with them. You make that person become fond of you, and this makes them trust you. This mirroring of their actions creates a mutual understanding. This technique is very effective in social and professional settings where you are required to build connections. If the person you are talking with leans forward and places their hands on the table, doing the same can make them feel more comfortable. However, you should do it subtly to avoid appearing insincere or mocking.

- **Proxemics:** This is the study of personal space—the distance you create between yourself and others. This space communicates a lot about your relationship and comfort level with others. Standing too close to someone you've just met can make them feel uncomfortable or threatened, while standing too far away from a friend can signal disinterest or detachment. Understanding the appropriate amount of personal space in different contexts helps you communicate with respect and attentiveness. In Western cultures, for example, personal space tends to be larger, while in some other cultures, closer proximity is more acceptable and even expected.

- **Eye contact:** This is one of the most powerful nonverbal communications. It can show your interest, attention, confidence, and sincerity toward others. It is a sign of engagement and focus when you keep your eyes on the person you are speaking to. This helps build trust between the two of you. However, you should not look at them for too long because it may make them feel uncomfortable. On the other hand, avoiding eye contact shows that you are not interested or feel insecure in that person's presence.

- **Touch and intimacy:** Touch is a very important way of interacting with someone. It communicates various emotions and messages, from comfort and affection to dominance and aggression. The context and the nature of the touch give it meaning. When you gently touch someone on the arm, you are showing empathy and support, while a firm handshake can convey confidence and professionalism. However, you should be aware of cultural differences and personal boundaries when it comes to touch. In many cultures, physical touch is a common part of communication, while in others, it is reserved for close relationships. When you take this into consideration, you can use touch appropriately to strengthen your relationships with others.

The Art of Reading Body Language

You need to develop this skill of being able to read body language if you want to improve your relationships and the way you communicate with others. You can read body language when you follow the following steps:

First, you need to understand the various nonverbal cues people use to communicate. Each of the nonverbal cues mentioned in the previous section can communicate something about a person, whether their feelings or intentions. For instance, crossed hands may mean defensiveness or discomfort, while open palms show honesty and openness. Maintaining eye contact may mean someone is interested in you or engaged in what you are saying, whereas avoiding eye contact may mean someone is shy or evasive. When you pay attention to such signals, you can easily understand the underlying emotions and thoughts of the people you interact with.

Then, you have to be able to recognize universal signals. When you read and recognize such signals, you can accurately interpret basic emotions and intentions. There are many of these signals, but they are simple to understand. Familiarizing yourself with such common gestures and expressions gives you the ability to communicate with people from different backgrounds more effectively. It also gives you an understanding of how you should approach different people.

To effectively interpret universal signals, you need to analyze the context behind them. If a person crosses their arms in a cold room, it means they are trying to stay warm instead of feeling defensive. When someone avoids eye contact while in a serious conversation with you, this means they are thinking but not being dishonest. Hence, when conducting contextual analysis, consider the surrounding environment, the nature of the interaction, and the individual's baseline behavior before coming to a conclusion.

If you are to read body language effectively, you must also be a keen observer. To be good at observation during everyday situations, such as meetings, social gatherings, or even while watching television shows, you should pay close attention to other people's facial expressions, gestures, and postures. Try to imagine what they may be feeling at that time based on these nonverbal cues. When you keep practicing this, reading the simple signals people give off will be easy. You can also improve at observation when you try monitoring your own body language and imagining how others may perceive it.

Techniques for Analyzing Behavior

Do you want to understand someone's actions, motivations, and thought processes? You can understand these if you analyze and truly understand their behavior. There are many techniques you can use to analyze people's behavior.

Behavioral Patterns

You have to pay attention to the recurring actions, reactions, and habits this person exhibits. When you recognize and analyze the patterns, you will get to know a lot of information about them and their behavior—personality, preferences, and what motivates them to do what they do. I once had a friend who could report to meetings late almost every day, and when the time came for him to discuss his opinions, he could avoid eye contact. What these patterns told me was that he was a shy person who was not confident in his ideas. If you find out these patterns, you can easily anticipate how someone will respond in different situations. If they are going through hard times and are stressed, you can easily tell from the deviation from typical behavior. You will notice someone who has been appearing confident starting to isolate themself.

Psychological Profiling

This is where you assess the psychological characteristics, including personality traits, cognitive abilities, and emotional tendencies, of someone.

This technique helps you predict their behavior and understand the reasons behind their actions. This is mostly used in fields such as law enforcement to create profiles of suspects and understand their modus operandi. When doing this, you collect all the information you can get about someone's behavior, personality, and cognitive patterns. After that, you examine this data to acquire a better knowledge of their preferences, strengths, shortcomings, and personality features. This helps you understand why they do what they do. Besides being used in law enforcement, you can use it in hiring, team building, or conflict resolution.

When I was a company manager, it was always my role to improve team dynamics. One day, I noticed that a team member called Alex always wanted to work independently and used to avoid social gatherings. This was the first time I had to do psychological profiling—on him. With some digging, I discovered that Alex was an introvert who lived in structured environments and valued deep, uninterrupted work. Knowing this, I had to change my management style toward him. I started giving Alex more solo projects and quieter workspaces. I also gradually suggested including him in team activities. I did this in a way that didn't overwhelm him. This actually made him more productive. All this was possible because I understood his strengths and addresses.

Questioning Techniques

When gathering information about someone, make sure you ask the right questions. Such questions get you the correct answers. What do I mean by the right questions? Make sure you ask open-minded questions. These may lead to a wider conversation, and you may end up getting all you would love to know about someone. Such questions may include, "Can you tell me more about your experience with…?" "What inspired you to take this career path?" or "How do you usually go about challenges in your work?"

Also, by the right questions, I mean you can ask about specific issues such as:

- "What are some of the biggest challenges you face in your role?"
- "How do you manage stress when dealing with tight deadlines?"
- "Can you describe a recent project that you found particularly rewarding or difficult?"

Being thoughtful is a must if you want to ask strategic questions. However, you should avoid leading or biased questions. For instance:

- **Leading:** "Don't you think the new policy is unfair?"
    - **Better:** "What are your thoughts on the new policy?"
- **Leading:** "Isn't it true that our team is the best?"
    - **Better:** "How would you describe our team's strengths and areas for improvement?"
- **Leading:** "You agree that this project is a waste of time, right?"
    - **Better:** "What are your perspectives on the value of this project?"

Moreover, you must consider the context and purpose of your inquiry, as well as the individual's personality and communication style.

Considerations in Interpretation

We have been talking about how important it is to analyze and interpret information, whether from conversations, written texts, or observed behaviors. Before you engage in interpretation, what are the key considerations to keep in mind?

Avoiding Assumptions

Usually, assumptions end relationships. How? You see, when you assume why someone has said or done something, you are likely to misunderstand and misinterpret them. The fact is, no one would know the reason apart from themself or sometimes the people around them. You need to know the whole story first. It's very risky to go with what you think it is. You end up getting it all wrong. But if you took time to clear up those assumptions, you would have gotten the message in its original context. If you want to avoid this, look for clarification when you don't understand something. Be open-minded and ask as many questions as you want. You will get various perspectives, which you can analyze and interpret to get the correct information or message.

Cultural Sensitivity

People have different cultural backgrounds. Remember, each culture has its own communication norms, values, and beliefs. Because of this, you may find people communicating in a certain way. Before you interpret anything, acknowledge the existing cultural differences, and always try your best to respect and understand others. When you find someone with a different culture from yours, don't impose your cultural biases on them. Don't interpret things as if you are talking to someone from your own culture. Be respectful, mindful, curious, and empathetic.

Respecting

Acknowledge the dignity and worth of those around you, even though they have different opinions from yours. Actively listen when they are talking, make eye contact, and avoid interrupting them. This is how you can show respect to someone, even if you disagree with them. Show them that you understand what they are feeling or going through. You should also prioritize confidentiality and privacy when dealing with information about someone else.

Questioning Biases

When interpreting something, you will definitely engage in introspection and also have to question your own biases and assumptions. If you dare interpret information when you are biased, whether conscious or unconscious, you are likely to make unfair judgments or misinterpretations. To get rid of the biases, seek out different perspectives and carefully analyze them. Be curious; whatever you do not understand, ask for facts. When you do this, you will come to more accurate conclusions.

Using Insights for Enhanced Communication

Communication is very important in all relationships, whether personal or professional. To improve the way you communicate with others, you must consider some key insights. When you implement these insights, you will see various aspects of communication improve.

Tailoring Communication Styles

How you communicate with one person is different from the way you should communicate with another. People are different. If you communicate using the same style with different people, you will be perceived in different ways. Some may be welcoming, while others may feel irritated. The way I want to be talked to is not what another person wants. It's your responsibility to find out how. Some people want you to be more direct and assertive, while others may respond better to a more empathetic and nurturing approach. When you observe and adapt to individual preferences, you will shape your message to resonate with your audience. To know how you are perceived, pay critical attention to their verbal and nonverbal cues as they are talking or interacting with you. This will help you understand what each of these people prefers and what you can change to make them feel comfortable with you. It can be adjusting your tone, language, and delivery style—whatever it is, as long as it aligns with what they want. Is someone reserved or introverted? You may want to use a more gentle and supportive approach to encourage open dialogue.

Building Trust

For any relationship to thrive, you must have trust as its foundation. Trust is built by being consistent with what you do and say. Being viewed as a credible and reliable person is gauged by your consistency. When talking to others, be transparent and authentic. When you make any commitments, it should be a must for you to follow through on them. Any small traces of dishonesty may break trust. Thus, promise what you know you can fulfill. It is easy to build trust but easier to break it. Be honest, have integrity, and respect others for a strong relationship.

Conflict Resolution

Conflicts occur every day in relationships. How you resolve them determines how long your relationship will last. Conflicts usually come from miscommunication, misunderstandings, or differing views or opinions. When it arises in your relationship, you should be willing to listen to what the other person has to say. And you do not just listen; you have to make sure you come to a mutual understanding. Do not interrupt or place blame on them. You should only focus on finding common ground together. Avoid things that may escalate the situation. In the end, you will get the best solution to the issue.

Key Points

- Facial expressions, body language, eye contact, gestures, and physical distance are nonverbal ways to communicate.

- Recognizable facial expressions, such as happiness, sadness, and anger, make it easier for someone to understand you.

- Confident body language, such as upright posture, signals authority, while slouched posture may convey submission or discomfort.

- Mimicking the body language of others builds rapport and fosters trust.

- Do not encroach on someone's personal space.

The next chapter explores seduction and emphasizes the importance of suspense, mystery, and emotional connection in the process, ultimately stressing the balance between authenticity and the strategic use of deception to achieve personal and professional goals in relationships.

CHAPTER 9

Crafting Irresistible Charisma

—

Strategies for Captivating Hearts and Minds

Life can show up no other way than that way in which you perceive it.

– NEALE DONALD WALSH

Understanding the Psychology of Attraction and Seduction

Attraction and seduction are fascinating aspects of human behavior. They come from both psychological and biological mechanisms.

Exploring the Evolutionary Basis of Attraction

Attraction is about survival and reproduction. When they say you are attractive, it means people are effortlessly drawn toward you. This may be because you have traits that they like. These traits may signal health, fertility, and the potential for strong offspring. If you are attracted to someone who has clear skin, symmetrical features, and a healthy physique, you are subconsciously looking at this person as one with good genetics and health.

If you are drawn to someone with broad shoulders and a confident stance, what these features reveal to you is that this person is physically strong and able to protect and provide. These qualities make them attractive. Also, getting drawn to someone with a nurturing demeanor shows that they are likely to be potentially supportive and caring partners, which are important qualities when raising children.

Psychological Theories of Attraction

The reason why you are attracted to someone is explained more by psychological theories. One of the most popular theories is the similarity-attraction effect. This implies that you are more likely to find people attractive if they have comparable backgrounds, values, and interests. This is because it is very easy to trust someone with whom you share your love for hiking, your passion for environmental conservation, and your favorite music genre. These create a common ground where you can easily relate to each other and make you feel more comfortable and secure when you are with them. Hence, this is the reason you are attracted to them. I became friends with someone because we supported the same soccer club. I was attracted to my first girlfriend because she was a wrestling fan. There are many things that can draw you to someone.

Another theory we can consider is the reward theory of attraction. This means that you are essential to someone because they provide you with rewarding experiences. If you find yourself feeling good, appreciated, and happy when you are with someone, trust me, you are likely to get fond of them. You are going to be strongly attracted to that person. If you went on a date with someone and they made you laugh endlessly or were very kind and thoughtful with you, these feelings are what will boost your attraction to them.

Acknowledging the Impact of Social and Cultural Elements

Does your social and cultural environment affect your perception of attractiveness? Yes. Cultural norms and societal standards significantly affect what draws you to someone. In some cultures, a person with a fuller body figure is considered more attractive because they are believed to be wealthy and healthy, which is not the case in other cultures that prefer slimmer physiques.

Fashion trends also affect your sense of attraction. When living in a society where high-end fashion and grooming are greatly valued, you are likely to be drawn to those with a polished appearance and who dress well. Similarly, suppose your social media feeds or Facebook page (FYP) are full of influencers and celebrities with certain body types, styles, or lifestyles. In that case, your ideals of beauty are likely to be based on who you follow. However, if you grew up in an environment where kindness and generosity were highly valued, you will always find these qualities the most attractive. This shows that personal experiences also affect your attraction patterns.

Exploring the Role of Hormones

Biologically, you can get attracted to someone. Let me explain. Our bodies produce hormones, such as dopamine, oxytocin, and serotonin, often referred to as the *feel-good* hormones, that influence our feelings of attraction and seduction.

When you feel attracted to someone, your body releases dopamine, which makes you very excited. This is the reason behind that feeling of happiness when you see a text from someone you're interested in or when you're on an exciting first date.

Then, we have oxytocin—the love hormone. This is the one that causes bonding and attachment. It is released when you physically touch the person you are attracted to, such as hugging, kissing, or holding hands. This hormone is why you may feel very close to someone after a warm embrace or a gentle caress.

In sexual attraction, there are testosterone and estrogen. Testosterone is more common in males. This hormone makes them more confident and assertive when pursuing a partner. Estrogen, which is at high levels in females, enhances the features that men are attracted to.

Subliminal Factors That Trigger Attraction

These factors include:

Attitude

Having a positive attitude makes you magnetic. Being optimistic tells others you are approachable, confident, and capable of handling anything. This will draw many people toward you and make you more appealing. With a positive attitude, you show interest in others and what they have to say, which makes you more attractive.

A quick question: If you go to a party and find two kinds of people. One who wears a smile, compliments others sincerely and shows enthusiasm while engaging with other people, and another with a negative attitude who always complains or criticizes; who would you feel comfortable approaching?

Having a bad attitude scares people away. It blocks many great opportunities from coming your way. If you are in a job interview and display a positive and can-do attitude, you are likely to get that job, unlike your colleague with a negative attitude.

Confidence

Being confident shows that you believe in yourself and your abilities. This is very attractive because it communicates to others that you are competent and reliable and you know what you want.

In your personal life, displaying confidence makes you more attractive. If you're on a date, for example, speaking confidently about your interests and experiences can make you more appealing to your date. Confidence in your body language, such as standing tall and maintaining eye contact, can further enhance this effect. Note that confidence doesn't mean being arrogant; it's about having a healthy level of self-esteem and presenting yourself authentically.

Body Language

There are many ways your body language can trigger attraction. Having positive body language makes you appear more friendly and engaging. If you maintain eye contact when talking to someone, it shows that you are interested and attentive. This tends to make them feel more comfortable with you because you make them feel valued and understood. Also, a genuine smile is another attractive trait. A smile shows that you are inviting, and this makes people feel at ease around you.

Let's say you are in a meeting. If you sit with an open posture, maintain eye contact, nod in agreement, and use hand gestures to emphasize points, your audience will likely trust what you're saying more. This won't be the case if you cross your arms or avoid eye contact.

Recognizing When Seduction Crosses Ethical Boundaries

Ethically, seduction must involve mutual consent, genuine attraction, and honesty. When seduction doesn't involve any of those or starts steering into manipulation, coercion, or deceit, it becomes unethical. If someone pretends to share your interests just to win your attention or affection, they are being unethical. This leads to distrust and, eventually, emotional harm.

So, how can you distinguish between natural attraction and deceptive methods? When your attraction toward someone is based on mutual respect, shared interests, and honest communication, that is genuine attraction. This shows that it is authentic and sincere. However, if you have to involve manipulation and deceit for someone to get drawn to you, that's deceptive. Excessively flattering someone, making various promises, and creating a false sense of urgency in the relationship are some of the deceptive methods that can be used. If the attraction is real, you don't need any tactics; it grows naturally.

There are many signs you can use to identify deceptive seduction methods. The first one is inconsistency. If you find that someone constantly changes their narrative or acts in different situations, you should be careful with them because they may be hiding their true intentions. Another warning sign is pressure to move the relationship forward quickly. Ethical seduction does not need to be rushed; its progress is natural. You may find this person creating a sense of urgency or scarcity in trying to rush the relationship. This is a red flag.

Be careful when you notice any traces of manipulation, like using manipulative language. If this person often uses statements such as, "If you really loved me, you would…" or, "You're the only one who understands me," they are trying to make you emotionally dependent on them. Furthermore, you have to pay close attention to how the person reacts when you assert your boundaries. If your partner is ethical, they will respect your limits. A deceptive one might try to guilt-trip you or persuade you to ignore them.

Examining the Psychological Dynamics of Seduction

These dynamics involve the relationships between attraction, desire, and emotional manipulation. In ethical seduction, attraction and desire are used in a way that respects the autonomy and consent of the people involved. This approach is entirely based on an honest and genuine connection. In such a relationship, both parties benefit.

On the other hand, deceptive seduction exploits your psychological weaknesses, such as self-esteem, insecurities, and the natural human need for connection. They may use different kinds of manipulative techniques based on your vulnerabilities. They want to ensure you are no longer confident or lack self-esteem. This will make you dependent on them, which makes it easy to trick you into whatever they want you to do.

In summary, intentions determine whether seductive behavior is ethical or deceptive. When someone has pure and good intentions toward you, they will respect your boundaries and be honest about their feelings and intentions. However, someone with bad intentions may use a deceptive and unethical approach.

Honing Authentic Charisma and Magnetism

To have authenticity in your charisma and magnetism, you have to make sure you are the best version of yourself. Authentic charisma isn't about putting on a show. You have to let your true self shine in an attractive way.

Developing Sincere Self-Assurance and Confidence

To build your self-assurance and confidence, you must first accept yourself as you are. You have to believe in yourself. You need to know your strengths and weaknesses, and you have to embrace them fully. Moreover, you have to be comfortable with who you are and all that you are capable of offering. Oprah Winfrey had a difficult childhood, but look at what she has become. She believed in herself. She never pretended to be someone she was not. Deep in her heart, she knew confidence is never about failing; it's just the belief that you can handle whatever comes your way. You have to believe in your abilities. If you want to learn how to gain more confidence and self-assurance, you can recheck the previous chapters.

Gaining Charming Communication Abilities

To communicate with charisma, you need to listen attentively, understand what is being said, and then respond in a way that makes the other person feel heard and valued. It is not just about speaking well. You have to pay close attention to someone when talking and not interrupt or try to respond to them. You should ask follow-up questions for more understanding. In addition, your body language must show that you are interested. An example is Barack Obama. He is a very appealing person because of his great and charming communication abilities. He listens intently, responds thoughtfully, and uses his words to inspire and unite people. Whenever he is talking, it always feels like he is connecting or creating a bond with you.

Accepting Authenticity and Vulnerability in Relationships

You need to show your true self to others and be open about your feelings and experiences. This can be quite challenging because it requires you to trust someone highly. According to Brené Brown, a researcher and storyteller, genuine connection comes from allowing ourselves to be seen—really seen. You have to be confident enough to share your own struggles and imperfections to grow a strong bond with others. You have to share your joys, fears, and disappointments. This makes someone trust you. Eventually, your relationship will become stronger.

Using Your Own Advantages to Naturally Draw Others

You can also use your own advantages to attract others naturally. This means you can use your unique skills, talents, and characteristics to be attractive. You have to know that everyone has something unique to offer, whether it's a talent or a passion. Steve Jobs was not the most technically skilled person at Apple, but he used his vision and innovative thinking to revolutionize the tech industry. Because of his unique ability to see the big picture and inspire others to follow his vision, he managed to create one of the biggest tech companies.

His charisma came from his passion and ability to communicate his ideas effectively.

You have to identify your unique strengths, such as storytelling, a talent for organizing, or a passion for helping others, and find ways to use them in your interactions with others. When you focus on these strengths, you can use them authentically.

Ethical Savvy Seduction Techniques

To ethically be seductive, you can use the following techniques:

- **Fostering a genuine connection:** If you really want to build a genuine connection with someone, you have to put all your focus on creating a meaningful bond. You have to look beyond superficial charm. For a genuine bond to happen, you must have a true interest in the other person's life, passions, and values. What I mean is that instead of just using mere rehearsed pick-up lines or trying to impress someone with flashy gestures, you have to ensure you deeply know and bond with someone. This happens by building trust through sharing personal stories, asking thoughtful questions, and actively engaging in conversations that reveal your true self. For example, if you meet and get drawn to someone, ask them about their interests instead of trying to impress them with exaggerated stories of your accomplishments. You must be curious about the subject if they tell you that they love painting. Ask them about what inspires their art. Talk about how some specific artist's work intrigues you. When you do this, you will develop a deep mutual conversation. This makes you develop a deeper connection with someone.

- **Active listening and empathy:** You have to be entirely empathetic, and you have to actively listen to what they have to say. Doing this makes them trust you more because they feel you understand them. In case your partner had a bad day, and they are trying to tell you how the day went, don't ignore them; listen to them attentively. You may also tell them, "It sounds like you had a really tough day. That must have been frustrating." This shows that you understand them, and it deepens your relationship.

- **Mutual respect and consent:** Respect and consent from both parties are signs of a healthy partnership. To do this, you have to treat people the way you want to be treated. You must also honor their bounds. Never make them do anything uncomfortable under duress. After a successful date, you begin to feel attracted to each other. You have to politely inquire, "I really enjoy spending time with you and feel a strong connection. How do you feel about taking this further?" This allows the other individual to voice their thoughts about it. This shows you care for them.

- **Transparency and honesty:** Openness about your intentions, feelings, and expectations builds trust. If you are honest from the start, you avoid misleading the other person. If you find yourself dating someone but, at that time, you're not ready for a serious relationship, you can honestly and respectfully tell them. You can say, "I really enjoy spending time with you, and I want to be clear that I'm not looking for a long-term commitment right now. I hope that's okay with you." This prevents misunderstandings and ensures both parties are on the same page.

Navigating Power Dynamics and Gender Norms in Seduction

To have a healthy relationship, you and your partner must have mutual respect, shared decision-making, and challenge traditional gender roles. An example of such a relationship is between Michelle and Barack Obama. Michelle has talked openly about how their relationship has been a partnership of equals, with both supporting each other's careers and personal growth. She said that even when Barack became president, she didn't simply conform to the traditional role of the First Lady. She actively went on to pursue her own goals. This made her a solid and independent figure. In this setting, you can use power dynamics to have a healthy and respectful relationship in many ways.

First, you have to take conventional gender roles and stereotypes to task. These dictate how you should behave in romantic and sexual contexts. As a man, you are expected to initiate romantic or sexual encounters, and you must be assertive and dominant. As a woman, you are expected to wait for the man to make the first move. Following these stereotypes may lead to unhealthy dynamics because they tend to limit your ability to express yourself. But what would happen if you broke them? My wife took the initiative to ask me out for coffee. This meant that she stepped outside the traditional gender role. This showed how confident she was. And I believe she felt empowered. On my end, I felt relieved. I appreciated her straightforwardness. I didn't have to take on the burden of initiation alone. I can't lie; I enjoyed the dynamic of someone else taking the lead for a change, and I respected her for that.

Then, you have to enable others to make knowledgeable decisions regarding romantic activities. This is very important in a relationship. Ensure that all the other people involved have a clear understanding of what their choices mean and the consequences of their actions. This means that the relationship must have healthy communication and mutual consent. Before going deeper into your relationship, you should have a conversation with your partner about boundaries and expectations. This shows that you respect each other.

Power imbalances are common in relationships and originate from factors such as age, experience, social status, or emotional dependency. If you want to maintain a respectful and equitable relationship, it is important to be aware of and sensitive to these dynamics. When you are dating someone significantly younger or less experienced than you, you have to make sure that your partner feels heard and valued. You should not make decisions alone. A relationship involves two people, and you must always check in with your partner to know their opinion. This makes them comfortable with the relationship. Resist the temptation to dominate the relationship.

You should also encourage parity and respect for one another in relationships. You have to make sure that everyone feels valued and equal. You have to listen to each other, make decisions together, and share your responsibilities. For instance, in a household, traditional gender roles suggest that women should handle most of the domestic work. You can decide to change the norm by sharing the roles in a way that feels fair to both of you. This shows teamwork and mutual respect.

Key Points

- Attraction is rooted in survival and reproduction, where traits signaling health and fertility, like clear skin and symmetrical features, are deemed attractive.

- The similarity-attraction effect explains that people are drawn to those with similar interests and values, which creates trust and comfort.

- Cultural norms and societal standards define what we perceive as attractive, such as body type preferences and fashion trends.

- Hormones like dopamine, oxytocin, and testosterone affect feelings of attraction and bonding.

In the next chapter, you'll learn how to leverage persuasion in business, emphasizing honesty, empathy, and transparency, and illustrating how aligning with stakeholders' beliefs can yield desired results, providing readers with tools for moral decision-making, creating strong relationships, and achieving mutually beneficial outcomes in modern business.

CHAPTER 10

Strategic Influence

—

Leveraging Persuasion in Business

Nothing in the world is so compelling to the emotions as the mind of another human being.

— MARGARET FLOY WASHBURN

Persuasive Sales Techniques

The number of sales you make shows what a good salesperson you are. Your business grows with an increasing number of sales. But how do you get customers? Through persuasion. Competition is normal business. Everyone wants customers to buy their product. So, you have to be very good at attracting as many buyers as you can. Your persuasive power must be top-notch. If you want to be good at persuasion, you can use the following techniques:

- **Building trust:** Before anything else, for someone to buy from you, they must trust you. Therefore, you have to make this person trust you and make sure the client feels confident about you. You have to make them feel like you have their best interests at heart. To build trust, you must show you are honest, reliable, and transparent in all your interactions. Trust is crucial because customers today are more informed and skeptical than ever before. You should be patient when dealing with your clients; do not push them into making decisions. You have to listen to the client attentively and answer all their queries honestly. You have to provide all the necessary information for them to understand what you are selling. You have to show that you understand what you are selling. If there are any other models or alternatives to that particular product, share them with them and tell them the differences. This is how you win someone's trust.

- **Value-based selling:** You have to make sure that you understand the specific needs and desires of the client. It is these that you have to address. This means that instead of focusing on the features of a product, you have to put much emphasis on what value the product brings to the customer. Before selling anything to someone, first understand their challenges. Then, tell them how your product is the solution. For instance, if you are selling a software product to a client, rather than jumping into its features like task tracking and time logging, you have to do some research and understand their pain points. Suppose you discover that their challenges are missed deadlines and poor team communication. In that case, you have to explain how your software can improve their workflow efficiency and collaboration, saving them time and money.

- **Consent-oriented approach:** When using this approach, you have to gain permission from the customer at each stage of the sales process. This makes them feel in control and less pressured to make decisions. If you are a financial advisor, you can ask the client if they are interested in discussing their financial goals. When you finish providing the initial advice, you can ask them if they are okay with you presenting a detailed plan at that moment. When you keep asking for their consent to proceed, it keeps them on board and also makes them comfortable with you. This approach makes the client feel valued and respected, and they will end up trusting you.

- **Long-term relationship-building:** This strategy requires building a long-lasting relationship with your client. This means continuously engaging with clients and giving them updates on the ongoing value. Even after the sale is made, you can keep in contact with them, ensuring they are satisfied or even asking for the status of the product. Doing this turns one-time buyers into loyal customers and brand advocates.

Navigating Workplace Dynamics With Integrity

Creating a workplace built on integrity is not entirely about following rules. You have to make sure that every individual feels respected, valued, and motivated to contribute their best. Doing this requires dedication and mindfulness. There are many ways you can create this kind of workplace, and they include the following:

Firstly, you have to promote a culture of ethics. As a leader or employee, you have to show integrity in whatever you do. This creates a healthy and productive work environment. And doing this sets a precedent for others to follow. If you are always transparent when making decisions, others will be influenced to do the same. Also, openly discussing the rationale behind decisions, even when they are tough, makes you a trusted and respected figure among your peers.

Moreover, you have to ensure fair treatment of employees. This boosts their morale and loyalty within your team. Fair treatment means you have to provide equal growth opportunities and address unjust or unfair treatment. This can involve an equitable distribution of resources, transparent decision-making processes, and unbiased performance evaluations. You have to create an environment where all the employees feel they have something to contribute to the company.

How you handle conflicts determines the atmosphere of your organization. When solving conflicts, you should be fair in your judgment. Make sure you listen to both sides and then find a mutually acceptable solution. You should address the conflict head-on as soon as you identify it; never let it escalate. Furthermore, being able to make persuasive decisions is a valuable skill. To be good at this, you have to present your ideas and decisions in a way that others can understand and support. You have to be good at logical reasoning, emotional intelligence, and effective communication. A persuasive leader can present his ideas in such a way that everyone views them as the only option. This skill can attract many investors to a business.

Lastly, you have to ensure whistleblower protection. This means that employees are free to speak up, guaranteeing their freedom to report any wrongdoing without fear of retaliation. Having this policy in place encourages a transparent and accountable workplace. It protects potential whistleblowers from intimidation, threats, coercion, harassment, and discrimination. However, you have to emphasize that the whistleblower reports issues through proper channels.

Fostering Genuine Connections in Professional Settings

In professional settings, creating genuine connections means more customers or investments in your business. Creating and maintaining this relationship is not just about swapping pleasantries or collecting contacts like trading cards; it's also about authenticity, active listening, emotional intelligence, bridging differences, and sincere communication.

- **Authentic networking:** Networking is often seen as a necessary evil in the professional world, but it doesn't have to be that way. You should handle every engagement with authentic curiosity when creating a genuine connection. You have to show that you really want to connect with this person. Hence, your intention should be to create a relationship that benefits both parties in the long run. Subsequently, share personal experiences and be vulnerable when you connect with someone on an authentic level. When interacting with them, show them respect and be truthful. Make sure you trust each other. You should also be willing to offer your time and expertise. Offer help and support without expecting anything in return, and you'll find that people are more willing to reciprocate.

- **Active listening:** In a genuine connection, you have to be able to understand each other. It is possible that you actively listen to your partner whenever they are saying anything. You have to pay extreme attention to the words coming out of them, their body language, and their tone of voice. Make eye contact, and make sure you ask relevant questions for clarity. This shows you are actually interested in what they are sharing and that you value their input. Allow them to finish speaking before you jump in to add your own thoughts or interrupt.

- **Emotional intelligence:** If you are emotionally intelligent, you are more likely to empathize with others, communicate clearly, and resolve conflicts constructively. This is possible if you are particularly self-aware, which means you truly understand your emotions and how they influence your thoughts and behavior. Being emotionally intelligent makes it easier for you to control your emotions, treat people with respect, and modify your communication style to fit various personalities and contexts. So, with this skill, you can easily interact with and understand each other in the workplace.

- **Building bridges across differences:** A workplace collects different people from different backgrounds. This leads to many cultural differences or even viewpoints and opinions. When dealing with such employees, you must be inclusive and collaborative. Be willing to learn from each other. You should understand that people with different ideas or who come from different places bring more innovative solutions. This is great for the company's growth. Create opportunities for employees with different experiences and viewpoints to collaborate and ensure everyone is given time to express themselves. This creates a more productive workplace.

- **Sincerity in business communication:** A genuine relationship is built on trust. Being sincere is very important if you want to be trusted. Whether delivering feedback, making promises, or expressing gratitude, you have to be honest and show integrity when communicating. Thus, avoid using vague or misleading language. When you are sincere, you show you are committed to building an authentic connection.

Influence Strategies

When convincing a friend, leading a team, or selling a product, you have to use some strategies to influence in order to be successful. Being influential is very important. These strategies include:

Convincing Others With Persuasion Techniques

When you aim to convince someone, you have to use persuasion techniques. First, you can use Aristotle's three modes of persuasion: ethos, pathos, and logos. Ethos is where you have to show that you are credible. After you show that you can be trusted and have expertise, people are more likely to listen to what you have to say. Then, pathos is where you use your emotional engagement with someone to connect with them. You can use stories, vivid language, and emotional triggers. Lastly, logos appeals to logic and reason. You should be clear and rational during arguments, and you should also make sure you provide evidence to make your case more concrete.

In addition, people tend to return favors when you do something for them. This is an effective trick: when you give someone a tip or a gift, they are more receptive to your requests. That's a fact.

People often look to others to decide how to act. You must show some proof that there are other people who support your idea through testimonials, reviews, and endorsements.

When convincing someone, you have to show them that what you are selling is scarce to increase its perceived value. When you show someone that an opportunity or product is rare, they will rush so they don't miss out.

Consensus Building

This technique brings about a general agreement in a group. This is particularly important in times when you are required to make decisions that may lead to the buy-in and cooperation of multiple stakeholders. If you want to build consensus effectively, you should follow these steps.

Begin by involving all those with a stake in the decision in the process. This makes them feel like their contribution and commitment are valued. Then, you have to encourage everyone to freely and comfortably share their views and concerns. Make sure everyone's views are respected. This promotes a productive discussion.

After listening to what everyone has to say, identify the common goals. Discuss what has been shared as a group and come to a common objective with which everyone agrees. This may reduce conflicts that may come up later on due to individual agendas. Then, you have to make sure that achieving this common goal is a team effort. Encourage the team to work together for the best results.

Besides, seek win-win solutions. You have to aim for outcomes that benefit everyone involved. A compromise is okay as long as all the stakeholders are happy and satisfied.

Authority and Credibility

You know that people will follow someone they know is an expert or credible source, right? What you have to do is establish yourself as that. But how? You have to show that you are an expert by sharing your qualifications, experiences, and successes. Have you published any articles or given talks about the field? Share that, too. As you associate with these people, you have to be a trustworthy, honest, transparent, and reliable individual.

When communicating, be clear, concise, and articulate. Make it easy for your audience to understand you. You must also look confident, dress appropriately, and maintain good body language. Furthermore, you can show proof of your expertise by sharing third-party endorsements and testimonials from respected figures in your field. In addition, it ensures having a strong professional network with other authorities and influential individuals. This makes other people more likely to trust you.

Storytelling

Storytelling is a powerful technique because it engages someone's emotions. It makes you more engaging, memorable, and persuasive. When telling a story, make sure you relate to your audience. First, conduct research on your audience and then tailor your stories to their experiences and interests. When someone visualizes themself in your story, connecting with what you are saying becomes very easy. When structuring your story, start with a compelling hook, build tension or conflict, and conclude with a resolution that reinforces your message. Make sure it is authentic and relatable. You can add sensory details and emotions to make your story come alive. And you should not forget the whole reason you are telling that story: the message. Make sure it aligns with the point you are trying to make.

Key Points

- To be successful in business, you have to build trust with clients, focus on value-based selling, use a consent-oriented approach, and prioritize long-term relationship building. Having these skills makes you persuasive enough to make more sales.

- Promote a culture of ethics, ensure fair treatment of employees, resolve conflicts effectively, make persuasive decisions, and protect whistleblowers to help navigate workplace dynamics with integrity.

- In case you want to connect genuinely with your professional partners, you should engage in authentic networking, practice active listening, utilize emotional intelligence, build bridges across differences, and communicate sincerely.

- Being an influential person requires using persuasion techniques, building consensus, establishing authority and credibility, and incorporating storytelling. These strategies help establish your presence.

The coming chapter examines the ethical use of personal influence, delving into power dynamics and moral considerations. It offers insights and strategies for using influence for positive impact and emphasizes accountability, empathy, and self-awareness to foster meaningful relationships and achieve positive outcomes in both personal and professional realms.

CHAPTER 11

Mindful Persuasion

—

Embracing Your Power of Magnetism

Great spirits have often overcome violent opposition
from mediocre minds.

– ALBERT EINSTEIN

Recognizing and Embracing Your Personal Power

Now that you are persuasive and have put all the tactics in the previous chapter into practice, do you recognize how magnetic you are? If not, don't worry. There are many ways you can identify this new-found personal power, and they include the following points:

First, do you know the sources of your own power? You see, personal power comes from various sources, both internal—such as your knowledge, skills, talents, experiences, and unique personality traits—and external—such as your relationships, network, and resources available to you. These internal sources are the personal assets that you bring to any situation, and you can use them to overcome any challenge and win over opportunities. Truly recognizing and understanding these sources helps you effectively use them. For instance, if you know you are great at communication, your leadership roles or negotiations will become easier. Another source of your power is your support system, such as friends and mentors. These people are your motivation and encouragement in many things you do. If no one supports you, there are many chances that you may fail.

When you reflect on your journey, how much have you achieved? Looking back through your past successes and achievements will help you identify patterns in your strengths, determination, and problem-solving skills. During self-reflection, do not forget the qualities and actions you had to change to get there. If you managed to complete a project, note down the skills you had to use, such as time management, creativity, or teamwork. This will help you know how much progress you have made in your journey of self-improvement.

At some point, you had self-limiting beliefs. Right? What are these beliefs? These are negative thoughts that block your potential or prevent you from achieving your goals. Usually, these beliefs or thoughts, such as *I'm not good enough, I'll never succeed,* or *I don't deserve happiness,* come from past experiences, societal expectations, or self-criticism. Recognize these thoughts, then replace them with positive ones. This is something you can do if you believe in yourself and your abilities. Do you ever believe *I'm not capable of leading a team?* To overcome it, think of the time you actually successfully managed to guide others or received positive feedback on your leadership skills. Having the power to reflect on and reframe negative beliefs or thoughts gives you a more empowering mindset.

Self-confidence is one of the best qualities you can have in life. It gives you a lot of opportunities. This is where you believe in your abilities and judgment. You can become confident by using positive beliefs or thoughts about yourself. These thoughts can help you overcome self-sabotaging and negative thoughts if you use them regularly. For example, telling yourself, *I am capable and strong; I have the skills needed to succeed,* or *I am worthy of my dreams* will make you feel nothing you start can fail. When using positive affirmations, they should be specific and in the present tense. Adding these to your daily routine gradually improves your self-perception.

Influencing Others Positively

Now that you are equipped with skills to influence others, how can you use them positively? Positively influencing someone involves guiding, motivating, and inspiring them to act, think, or feel in a way that leads to positive results. Do you want to learn how to do that? This is how:

You can lead by example. You have to live by the behaviors, attitudes, and work ethic you want to see in others. As a leader, consistently embodying the values and principles you advocate for sets a powerful standard. Do you want your colleagues to come early to work? Then, be punctual. Remember, actions speak louder than words. Instead of telling others to live a certain way, walk the talk. You will inspire others to follow suit, building credibility and trust in the team.

You should also be empathetic and good at listening. You have to be able to understand others to be able to influence them. Note that listening to them actively will help you understand them deeply. You will know their weaknesses and strengths. Your colleagues will feel valued and respected, and you will also be able to resolve conflicts and any misunderstandings that may arise. Trusting and following what you say will be easy for them.

Ensure a culture of transparency in your team or workplace. This is where everyone openly shares information, decisions, and feedback with others. Keep in mind that a transparent culture reduces rumors and misinformation. Establish a setting where people feel at ease talking about the rationale behind their choices, with a sense of being open to sharing triumphs and setbacks and being truthful about the difficulties they encounter. Regularly update the team on company goals, challenges, and progress. This can be done through town hall meetings, newsletters, and open-door policies. Encourage questions and provide honest answers. By doing so, trust is established, and everyone is working toward the same objective. This culture leads to a more engaged and committed workforce.

You can encourage collaboration and empower others. You can achieve collaboration through team-building activities and collaborative projects where ideas can be freely shared. Promote team projects and create cross-functional teams to tackle complex problems, providing the necessary resources and support for team members to succeed. In addition, recognize and reward collaborative efforts and individual contributions. When empowering others, you give them authority, resources, and autonomy to make decisions and take actions within their areas of responsibility. Establish clear goals and allow team members to take ownership of their tasks. This empowerment makes others more confident. These are key components of leadership that help your colleagues drive projects forward independently, which improves productivity.

Furthermore, you should respect diversity and inclusion. By respecting diversity, you acknowledge and appreciate the differences in people regardless of their backgrounds, opinions, and abilities. This makes everyone feel safe and comfortable. How can you do that? It's simple. All that's required is the implementation of equitable hiring procedures, providing diversity education, and promoting an inclusive work environment where everyone is valued equally.

Effective Communication Strategies

When you communicate, you want your intended message to be received accurately by the right people. However, before you communicate, there are many things you have to take into consideration:

- **Know your audience:** Well, you want to say something; to whom do you want to say it? If you want your message to be received and understood by many people, you have first to know who your audience is, what they know, what they need to know, and what they care about. Knowing this will enable you to communicate in a way that fits your audience's knowledge level, interests, and concerns. For instance, communicating with a group of experts on a technical subject is not the same as speaking to a general audience with little knowledge of the topic. You can look at its age, education level, cultural background, and prior knowledge and adjust your language, tone, and complexity accordingly.

- **Choose the right channel:** You need to choose the right channel for the message to be delivered effectively. These include face-to-face meetings, emails, phone calls, social media, printed materials, and more. They have different pros and cons. It's up to you to use what you feel will ensure your message is received the way you want it to be. Some messages require face-to-face communication, such as complex or sensitive information. For others, you can communicate through emails or messaging apps, such as giving out instructions. The choice depends on what you want to communicate.

- **Use clear and simple language:** Clarity and simplicity in language are essential for effective communication. Avoid jargon, technical terms, or overly complex sentences because they tend to confuse the audience. Always ensure your message is delivered in a way that is easy to understand. How can you achieve this? Use straightforward language and structure your message logically. Break down complex ideas into simpler components. Always use active voice instead of passive voice and concrete examples to clarify the message better. You may also use visual aids like charts or diagrams to improve your understanding.

- **Be respectful and empathetic:** This will earn you trust and rapport. Listen actively and show genuine interest in what others have to say. Use polite language and a considerate tone, especially when discussing sensitive or contentious issues. Showing respect and empathy creates a positive and supportive kind of communication, which leads to openness and collaboration.

- **Provide evidence and examples:** Supporting your message with evidence and examples improves clarity and credibility. It would be easy to influence someone because they feel you know what you are talking about. Data, statistics, research findings, expert testimonials, or real-life experiences can be evidence. Are you presenting a new business strategy? It is better for you to back your proposal with market research data, case studies of successful implementations, and specific examples of expected outcomes to receive positive feedback. They show the practical implications of your message.

- **Use feedback and follow-up:** Effective communication is a two-way process. You deliver the message, and then you critically listen to the audience. Asking for feedback helps you understand how accurately your message was received, and this enables you to know where to clarify. So, after communication, encourage feedback in the form of questions, comments, and suggestions, and be open to constructive criticism. After receiving the feedback, make sure you address any unresolved issues, clarify misunderstandings, and reinforce key points.

Building a Personal Brand Based on Authenticity and Integrity

Are you looking to be labeled as an authentic person with integrity? Make sure you align your outward persona with your true self, ensuring your actions, values, and words consistently reflect who you genuinely are. There is a lot to be considered to achieve this personal brand. First, you have to define your values. You should identify what truly matters to you—your values. It's these values that guide your behavior and decisions. Let them direct your actions and interactions. Do you want to be seen as honest and transparent? Make sure these two are evident in whatever you do, whether professionally or on a personal basis.

After defining your values, be consistent in your actions and words. Stand by what you advocate for. This makes you more reliable. If you want others to be punctual, consistently being on time reinforces this value. You are more likely to be respected and believed if you show a consistent behavior pattern that aligns with your values. You have to be consistent in all aspects of life. Then, ensure you are trusted and credible. You can be trusted if others can depend on you. Credibility comes from expertise, experience, and ethical conduct. To earn trust and credibility from others, be transparent about your capabilities and limits, admit mistakes, and take responsibility for your actions. You can also be seen as a credible person if you are willing to share knowledge or help others.

While maintaining core values and consistency is important, adapting and evolving are equally crucial. The world is constantly changing, and so should your personal brand. Well, do not change your values, but what you can change is how you express them. Stay informed about trends and feedback, and be open to growth and improvement. Doing this allows your brand to stay relevant and continue to relate to your audience. You can learn new skills, change your approach based on constructive criticism, or update your brand's visual and communication styles to better fit current trends.

Leveraging Influence for Positive Social Change and Impact

Creating a personal brand aims to gain enough power to initiate positive change. As your brand grows, so does your ability to influence others. You have to use this influence ethically to create and promote societal improvements. How?

- **Identifying opportunities for impact:** Look for areas where your influence can be most effective. This requires you to be informed about societal issues and understand community needs. For example, an underserved area with a lack of educational resources is an excellent opportunity for an entrepreneur willing to invest in schools or scholarships. Activists might see opportunities in policy reform, such as advocating for new laws that protect human rights. But you must be keenly aware of the problems and the possible solutions.

- **Advocating for justice and equality:** You can use your influence to actively support and promote policies, practices, and behaviors that ensure fair treatment and opportunities for all individuals. During this advocacy, you can campaign for legislative changes, raise public awareness, or support movements that fight against discrimination and inequality. You would have the goal of dismantling systemic barriers or issues, such as racial discrimination, gender inequality, and economic disparities, that prevent certain groups from achieving their full potential. You should be willing to be persistent, have a deep understanding of the issue, and be able to rally others to the cause.

- **Collaborating for collective impact:** You can work with various stakeholders—such as nonprofits, businesses, government agencies, and community groups—to achieve shared goals. Some issues cannot be solved individually, so coordinated effort is a better approach because it involves the strengths and resources of multiple partners. For instance, a coalition of nonprofits, government agencies, and private companies might come together to tackle homelessness, each contributing their unique strengths to create comprehensive solutions.

- **Inspiring others to action:** You can also use your influence to inspire others. Remember, inspiration is a powerful catalyst for change. You will be motivating and empowering people to take steps toward making a positive difference in their own lives and communities. You can achieve this through storytelling, leading by example, and creating a compelling vision for the future. Inspirational individuals lead by example. So, you have to be willing to be committed and passionate about what resonates with others. You can use your influence to galvanize support, mobilize volunteers, and encourage collective participation. You may also provide others with the tools, knowledge, and opportunities to contribute. This creates a sense of community and shared purpose in addressing social issues.

Key Points

- Identify the sources of your power, internal skills and experiences, and external relationships and resources to leverage them effectively in any situation.

- Reflect on past successes to recognize patterns in your strengths and problem-solving skills, fostering self-awareness and continuous self-improvement.

- Acknowledge and replace negative thoughts with positive ones to cultivate a more empowering mindset, boosting self-confidence and resilience.

- To positively influence and inspire others, lead by example, demonstrate empathy, promote transparency, encourage collaboration, and respect diversity.

- Tailor your message to your audience, choose the appropriate channels, use clear language, show respect and empathy, provide evidence, and seek feedback to ensure effective communication.

Conclusion

Throughout this book, we have deeply looked at what dark psychology looks like, how you can avoid it, and how you can use the power of being able to influence others positively. We studied different deceptive strategies commonly used in dark psychology and how you can easily identify and counteract them.

We have shed more light on manipulation and its common methods. We have outlined techniques for establishing boundaries and confronting manipulation head-on, equipping you with the knowledge to defend yourself and maintain healthy relationships. Furthermore, we highlighted the critical importance of awareness and critical thinking in avoiding being influenced by someone else when interacting with them.

On discussing the psychology behind the manipulative actions, we further learned how to strengthen mental toughness when faced with any kind of influence. We discovered activities that would help build our assertiveness and mental resilience. In addition, much emphasis has been put on the importance of being confident and having integrity. These help you preserve autonomy and protect personal boundaries against multiple kinds of manipulative behavior.

We explored how emotions affect human behavior. Here, we talked about key concepts like emotional intelligence, empathy, and motivation and how they affect human interactions and societal dynamics. This knowledge promotes harmonious coexistence, improved communication, and personal growth.

We further discussed the victim mindset and brainwashing techniques and how to defend yourself against them. This is where awareness and critical thinking were discussed as great defenses. Identifying manipulation, developing resilience, setting boundaries, mindfulness, and being assertive are great ways to escape victimization and being controlled by someone else.

We further learned about the ethical use of psychological strategies for personal betterment, balancing empowerment and domination. And lastly, you realized how you can interpret human behavior to predict actions. All that has been discussed shows how important it is to understand dark psychology.

So, with these tactics at your fingertips, you can protect yourself and others by creating healthy relationships. This shows the importance of having high awareness and critical thinking when dealing with others to avoid being manipulated and deceived. It is in your best interest to apply all the strategies that have been discussed to your daily life. At the end of the day, you will be able to attract more people than ever before.

I don't want you to think everyone is bad because they are not. Not at all.

In fact, most of us use some of the techniques detailed in the book in our day-to-day lives to a greater or lesser extent. The line between doing it ethically and morally and doing it wickedly is a matter of how aware or ignorant we are of the effects that our behaviors and actions can cause. Both for ourselves and others.

In this sense, we must recover our inner power to feel worthy and valuable for who we are. We must see all interactions and relationships with others as horizontal, not vertical.

To the extent that we recognize this inner sovereignty and learn to detect conscious or unconscious patterns that stem from dark psychology, we are indomitable. And that, dear friend, makes us magnets.

Magnets to attract our ideal partner.

Magnets to attract our boss or dream clients.

Magnets to attract our desired environment.

We no longer let any snake poison us.

Now, we are like a phoenix that enlightens other people.

A phoenix reborn and indomitable.

Your feedback is invaluable to us.

If you enjoyed the book, please leave an honest review or share your thoughts. Your input helps us improve future editions and ensures we continue to provide valuable content. We hope the insights gained have been enlightening and empowering. Stay vigilant, stay informed, and continue striving for integrity and transparency in all your interactions.

References

1. **Babic, B. (n.d.).** The flow psychology of attraction: A new turning point in learning how to naturally attract. Calameo. https://www.calameo.com/books/003336495fc8e89a15eef

2. **Bashir, S.** (2022, September 25). How to analyze people with dark psychology. Marstranslation. https://www.marstranslation.com/blog/how-to-analyze-people-with-dark-psychology

3. **Beasley, B.** (n.d.). Three strategies for ethical influence. Notre Dame Deloitte Center for Ethical Leadership. Ethicalleadership.nd.edu. https://ethicalleadership.nd.edu/news/is-the-moral-missing-from-your-message/

4. **Behaviors, emotions and feelings: How they work together.** (2023, April 23). Betterhelp. https://www.betterhelp.com/advice/behavior/behaviors-emotions-and-feelings-how-they-work-together/

5. **Birt, J.** (2019, December 12). The importance of emotional intelligence in the workplace. Indeed Career Guide. https://www.indeed.com/career-advice/career-development/emotional-intelligence-importance

6. **Blanco-Suarez, E.** (2018, March 21). The art of brainwashing. Psychology Today. https://www.psychologytoday.com/intl/blog/brain-chemistry/201803/the-art-brainwashing

7. **Boyd, N.** (2014). Self-understanding & self-concept: How we perceive ourselves. Study. https://study.com/academy/lesson/self-understanding-and-self-concept.html

8. **Brennan, D.** (2020, November 19). Manipulation: Symptoms to look for. WebMD. https://www.webmd.com/mental-health/signs-manipulation

9. **Buffalmano, L.** (2017, September 11). The art of seduction: 23 steps to seduce anyone. The Power Moves. https://thepowermoves.com/the-art-of-seduction/

10. **Buffalmano, L.** (2020, June 25). Dark psychology: 7 ways to manipulate people. The Power Moves. https://thepowermoves.com/dark-psychology/

11. **Building and maintaining healthy relationships.** (2021, October 27). Healthdirect Australia. https://www.healthdirect.gov.au/building-and-maintaining-healthy-relationships

12. **Building trust in relationships: A comprehensive guide to lasting connection.** (2024, February 13). Utah State University. https://extension.usu.edu/hru/blog/building-trust-in-relationships-guide-to-lasting-connection

13. **Cannon, J.** (2023, September 15). 3 red flags of the most manipulative people. Psychology Today. https://www.psychologytoday.com/intl/blog/stress-fracture/202308/3-ways-to-recognize-a-master-manipulator

14. **Cashin, A.** (2019, May 2). 21 recommended brain hacks from leading neuroscientists. Sainsbury Wellcome Centre. https://www.sainsburywellcome.org/web/blog/21-recommended-brain-hacks-leading-neuroscientists

15. **Cattel, R.** (n.d.). Raymond Cattel quotes. A-Z Quotes. https://www.azquotes.com/quote/1243292

16. **Cherry, K.** (2018, February 5). 8 basic psychology facts you need to know. Verywell Mind. https://www.verywellmind.com/psychology-basics-4157186

17. **Cherry, K.** (2023, February 23). Understanding body language and facial expressions. Verywell Mind. https://www.verywellmind.com/understand-body-language-and-facial-expressions-4147228

18. **Craig, H.** (2019, July 10). 10 ways to build trust in a relationship. Positive Psychology. https://positivepsychology.com/build-trust/

19. **Curi, I.** (2021, November 9). 7 smart ways to handle manipulation. LinkedIn. https://www.linkedin.com/pulse/7-smart-ways-handle-manipulation-ivna-curi

20. **Dennison, J.** (2023). Emotions: functions and significance for attitudes, behaviour, and communication. Migration Studies, 12(1). https://doi.org/10.1093/migration/mnad018

21. **Donald, N.** (n.d.). Neal Donald quotes. Goodreads. https://www.goodreads.com/author/quotes/9374.Neale_Donald_Walsch?page=6#:~:text=For%20you%20are%20the%20creator,which%20you%20think%20it%20will.&text=Father%2C%20help%20me%20never%20to,only%20upon%20the%20merit%20therein.

22. **Duggal, N.** (2018, July 13). Emotional intelligence in the workplace: Why you need it, how to get it. Simplilearn. https://www.simplilearn.com/emotional-intelligence-what-why-and-how-article

23. **Eatough, E.** (2022, February 1). 13 common red flags in a relationship to look out for. Betterup. https://www.betterup.com/blog/red-flags-in-a-relationship

24. **Einstein, A.** (n.d.). Albert Einstein quotes. Goodreads. https://www.goodreads.com/quotes/470750-great-spirits-have-always-encountered-violent-opposition-from-mediocre-minds

25. **5 magic steps to accurate body language: Mastering the art of nonverbal communication.** (2023, March 15). Bigvu. https://bigvu.tv/blog/5-magic-steps-to-accurate-body-language-mastering-the-art-of-nonverbal-communication

26. **Fracture, J.** (2022, June 20). Why do people manipulate? Psychology Today. https://www.psychologytoday.com/intl/blog/stress-fracture/202206/why-do-people-manipulate

27. **Frost, G.** (2023, April 1). Mastering the art of subliminal seduction: A guide to attracting women. Articles Factory. https://www.articlesfactory.com/articles/self-help/how-to-attract-women-using-subliminal-seduction-techniques.html#google_vignette

28. **Gautret, C.** (2017, August 8). The ethics of influence: Five rules to live. Learn to Influence. https://www.learntoinfluence.com/the-ethics-of-influence-five-rules-to-live-by/

29. **Gideon, Q.** (n.d.). Stop emotional manipulation | Trauma recovery. Woven Together Trauma Therapy. https://woventraumatherapy.com/blog/ways-to-protect-yourself-from-emotional-manipulation

30. **Gombos, R.** (2017, September 7). The art of reading body language and micro expressions. Jasmine Business Directory. https://www.jasminedirectory.com/blog/the-art-of-reading-body-language-and-micro-expressions/

31. **Green, R. K., & Pawlak, E. J.** (1983). Ethics and manipulation in organizations. Social Service Review, 57(1), 35–43. https://www.jstor.org/stable/30011611

32. **Gupta, S.** (2021, December 27). How to build trust in a relationship. Verywell Mind. https://www.verywellmind.com/how-to-build-trust-in-a-relationship-5207611

33. **Gupta, S.** (2023, November 13). How to protect yourself from emotional blackmail. Verywell Mind. https://www.verywellmind.com/emotional-blackmail-7974647

34. **Habtewold, A.** (n.d.). Assegid Habtewold quotes. Goodreads. https://www.goodreads.com/author/quotes/5324322.Assegid_Habtewold#:~:text=The%20people%20who%20would%20like,using%20them%20to%20their%20advantage.&text=When%20someone%20respects%20you%2C%20s,back%20and%20backbiting%20you...

35. **Hanselman, K.** (2023, October 27). Emotional manipulation tactics: Recognize and respond. Thriveworks. https://thriveworks.com/help-with/category/emotional-manipulation-tactics/

36. **Here's why you need ethical influence skills.** (n.d.). Martin John Training. https://www.martinjohn-training.com/blog/ethical-influence-skills-why-should-you-learn

37. **Hoffman, J.** (2019, January 15). What is "mind hacking" AKA metacognition? Medium. https://socialmediajosh.medium.com/what-is-mind-hacking-aka-metacognition-7ef6edbaf5c6

38. **Holland, M.** (2022, May 3). 17 manipulation tactics abusers use. Choosing Therapy. https://www.choosingtherapy.com/manipulation-tactics/

39. **Holtz, L.** (n.d.). Lou Holtz quotes. Brainy Quotes. https://www.brainyquote.com/quotes/lou_holtz_450789

40. **Houston, E.** (2019, February 6). The importance of emotional intelligence (including el quotes). Positive Psychology. https://positivepsychology.com/importance-of-emotional-intelligence/

41. **Hub, L. H.** (2023, June 29). The silent conversation: Mastering the art of body language. Medium. https://loveharmonyhub.medium.com/the-silent-conversation-mastering-the-art-of-body-language-8d204ee736e1

42. **The importance of building strong relationships with clients and colleagues.** (2023, February 13). AIContentfy. https://aicontentfy.com/en/blog/importance-of-building-strong-relationships-with-clients-and-colleagues

43. **Joel.** (2022, May 11). Dark psychology: The essential guide to master manipulators. Bloomsoup. https://bloomsoup.com/dark-psychology/

44. **Juhre, R. J.** (n.d.). Ralf Juhre quotes. Quote Ambition. https://www.quoteambition.com/manipulation-quotes/#google_vignette

45. **Kagan, J., & Lerner, R** (2020). Emotional development. Encyclopædia Britannica. https://www.britannica.com/topic/human-behavior/Emotional-development

46. **Lancer, D.** (2023, October 30). Mental health & relationships: Navigating manipulation in dating. Different Brains. https://differentbrains.org/mental-health-relationships-navigating-manipulation-in-dating/

47. **Langer, E. J.** (n.d.). Ellen J. Langer quotes. Goodreads. https://www.goodreads.com/quotes/1266261-it-is-not-primarily-our-physical-selves-that-limit-us

48. **LaVine, R.** (2023, March 21). Victim mentality: Signs, causes & 10 ways to break the cycle. Science of People. https://www.scienceofpeople.com/victim-mentality/

49. **Layton, J., & Hoyt, A.** (2006, May 10). How brainwashing works. How Stuff Works. https://science.howstuffworks.com/life/inside-the-mind/human-brain/brainwashing.htm

50. **Lebow, H.** (2022a, September 7). Victim mentality: Signs, causes, and what to do. Psych Central. https://psychcentral.com/health/victim-mentality

51. **Lebow, H.** (2022b, September 21). How to spot a manipulative person. Psych Central. https://psychcentral.com/lib/how-to-spot-manipulation

52. **Loyd, R.** (2023, August 10). A healthy relationship is built on a foundation of trust, respect, and mutual support. Medium. https://medium.com/@owengilbert8/a-healthy-relationship-is-built-on-a-foundation-of-trust-respect-and-mutual-support-c2178dd54544

53. **Macintosh, N. B.** (1995). The Ethics of profit manipulation: A dialectic of control analysis. Critical Perspectives on Accounting, 6(4), 289–315. https://doi.org/10.1006/cpac.1995.1027

54. **MS-HuecoDev.** (2023, November 19). Recognizing dark psychology in your daily life: Red flags and warning signs. Medium. https://medium.com/@mshuecodev/recognizing-dark-psychology-in-your-daily-life-red-flags-and-warning-signs-725f54c4eca8

55. **Murray, W.** (2021, August 25). Defense against mind control techniques and cult recruitment. Thriveworks. https://thriveworks.com/blog/protect-yourself-from-mind-control-techniques/

56. **Nagaraj, V.** (2021, February 11). Ethical influence. Psychology Today. https://www.psychologytoday.com/intl/blog/leading-in-the-real-world/202102/ethical-influence

57. **Notebaert, K.** (2020, August 14). What is brain hacking? How to use more of your brain. Insight Timer Blog. https://insighttimer.com/blog/how-to-hack-your-brain-for-full-potential-peak-performance/

58. **Oldford, S.** (2018, October 29). Manipulation in marketing: How It's used, and how to use it ethically. Entrepreneur. https://www.entrepreneur.com/growing-a-business/manipulation-in-marketing-how-its-used-and-how-to-use-it/321611

59. **Pattrick, W.** (2017, August 17). The seduction of secret—how intrigue sparks attraction. Psychology Today. https://www.psychologytoday.com/intl/blog/why-bad-looks-good/201708/the-seduction-secret-how-intrigue-sparks-attraction

60. **Perry, E.** (2022, August 4). How to control your mind: 10 tips to be your own champion. Betterup. https://www.betterup.com/blog/how-to-control-your-mind

61. **Prat, R.** (n.d.). Ron Prat quotes. Happier Human. https://www.happierhuman.com/manipulation-quotes/

62. **Raypole, C.** (2019, December 12). Victim mentality: 16 signs and tips to deal with it. Healthline. https://www.healthline.com/health/victim-mentality

63. **Raypole, C.** (2020, July 21). Family manipulation: Signs, tactics, and how to respond. Healthline. https://www.healthline.com/health/mental-health/family-manipulation

64. **Raypole, C.** (2021, January 8). How to control your mind: 10 techniques. Healthline. https://www.healthline.com/health/mental-health/how-to-control-your-mind

65. **Respect: trust and respect: The cornerstones of healthy relationships.** (n.d.). Faster Capital. https://fastercapital.com/content/Respect--Trust-and-Respect--The-Cornerstones-of-Healthy-Relationships.html

66. **Riehle, S.** (2022, March 18). Ethical selling: When does persuasion turn into manipulation? Zendesk. https://www.zendesk.com/blog/ethical-selling/

67. **Rooney, A.** (n.d.). Andy Rooney quotes. Goodreads. https://www.goodreads.com/quotes/132234-everyone-wants-to-live-on-top-of-the-mountain-but

68. **Sage, S.** (2023). 7 laws of dark psychology and manipulation: Gaslighting, NLP, love-bombing & covert persuasion -mastering art of emotional manipulation techniques to detect & defend yourself from dark psychology secret. Amazon Digital Services LLC - Kdp. https://books.google.com.bd/books/about/7_Laws_of_Dark_Psychology_and_Manipulati.html?id=qgGS0AEACAAJ&redir_esc=y

69. **Samuel.** (2023, February 6). How to understand people with dark psychology. Undergraduate Journal Of Psychology At Berkley. https://ujpb.org/dark-psychology/

70. **Sandison, H.** (2021, June 2). How to hack your mind - an interview with Sir John Hargrave. Qualia. https://qualialife.com/how-to-hack-your-mind-an-interview-with-sir-john-hargrave

71. **Sanyal, N.** (2021, October 26). How to manipulate customers… ethically. Harvard Business Review. https://hbr.org/2021/10/how-to-manipulate-customers-ethically

72. **The science of emotion: Exploring the basics of emotional psychology.** (2019, June 27). UWA Online. https://online.uwa.edu/news/emotional-psychology/

73. **Set boundaries against emotional manipulation.** (2024, March 6). Harvard Business Review. https://hbr.org/tip/2024/03/set-boundaries-against-emotional-manipulation

74. **Sheppard, S.** (2021, October 25). How to build a respectful relationship. Verywell Mind. https://www.verywellmind.com/respect-is-vital-to-building-a-healthy-relationship-5206110

75. **Simon, G.** (2009, April 13). Seduction as a manipulation tactic: Playing on your need to be valued. Counselling Resource. https://counsellingresource.com/features/2009/04/13/seduction-as-manipulation-tactic/

76. **Sinicki, A.** (2019, February 11). Human hacking - the art of reading body language. The Bioneer. https://www.thebioneer.com/human-hacking-art-reading-body-language/

77. **Sinusoid, D.** (2023, January 22). Understanding the psychology of seduction. Shortform Books. https://www.shortform.com/blog/psychology-of-seduction/

78. **Smith, J.** (2020, June 5). Ethical aspects of manipulation in marketing. Talk Business. https://www.talk-business.co.uk/2020/06/05/ethical-aspects-of-manipulation-in-marketing/

79. **Sparks, N.** (n.d.). Nicholas Sparks quotes. Goodreads. https://www.goodreads.com/quotes/132102-if-you-discovered-something-that-made-you-tighten-inside-you

80. **Stines, S.** (2017, July 11). Protecting yourself from manipulation. Psych Central. https://psychcentral.com/pro/recovery-expert/2017/07/protecting-yourself-from-manipulation#1

81. **The tactics of ethical influence.** (2021, December 15). A Berg's Eye View. https://abergseyeview.com/blog/2021/12/15/the-tactics-of-ethical-influence

82. **Team, M. S. T.** (2023, September 9). Top 10 dark psychology tricks for love. Mind Scape Today. https://www.mindscapetoday.com/2023/09/dark-psychology-tricks-for-love.html

83. **Travers, M.** (2024, March 29). How to defend yourself against manipulation. Psychology Today. https://www.psychologytoday.com/intl/blog/social-instincts/202403/how-to-defend-yourself-against-manipulation

84. **Turteltaub, A.** (2016, July 27). Influence others using leverage. The Compliance and Ethics Blog. https://www.complianceandethics.org/influence-others-using-leverage/

85. **Uddin, M.** (2019, May 31). Art of body language. Medium. https://medium.com/@merajpamir/art-of-body-language-there-are-basically-three-elements-in-communication-words-the-tone-of-295a67848ec0

86. **Vogel, K., & Craft, C.** (2022, April 15). 7 Manipulation tactics to know. Psych Central. https://psychcentral.com/lib/tactics-manipulators-use-to-win-and-confuse-you

87. **Washburn, M. F.** (n.d.). Margaret Floy Washburn quotes. Happier Human. https://www.happierhuman.com/manipulation-quotes/

88. **What does a healthy relationship look like?** (2017, January 31). New York State. https://www.ny.gov/teen-dating-violence-awareness-and-prevention/what-does-healthy-relationship-look

89. **What is a victim mentality?** (2021, March 30). WebMD. https://www.webmd.com/mental-health/what-is-a-victim-mentality

90. **Whitener, S.** (2022, December 30). Council post: Why is emotional intelligence important? Forbes. https://www.forbes.com/sites/forbescoachescouncil/2022/12/30/why-is-emotional-intelligence-important/?sh=737522f13289

91. **Younas, N.** (2024, January 27). Understanding the world of dark psychology: The dark arts of manipulation. Illumination. https://medium.com/illumination/understanding-the-world-of-dark-psychology-the-dark-arts-of-manipulation-4a03d5ae0925